PROPERTY LADDER

PROPERTY LADDER

HOW TO MAKE £££s FROM PROPERTY

Sarah Beeny with Philippa Ransford

This book is dedicated to my business partners in our development and investment companies and our property development consultancy company SGD Consulting Ltd (www.sgdconsulting.co.uk), Graham Swift and Diccon Beeny, without whose joint knowledge this book could not have been created. I thank them for all their support and for putting up with my absences during the filming of *Property Ladder*.

First published in Great Britain in 2002 by Cassell Illustrated, a division of Octopus Publishing Group Limited 2–4 Heron Quays, London E14 4JP

Reprinted 2002

Text by Sarah Beeny with Philippa Ransford
Editorial, design and layout by Essential Works

A CIP catalogue record for this book is available from the British Library.

ISBN 1 84403 022 9

Printed in Italy by Printer Trento S.r.l.

Contents

WHAT IS PROPERTY DEVELOPMENT?

This book is about property development and climbing the property ladder. It is not about simply redecorating your own home. To develop property means to buy a property and change it from one state to another. Done properly, this can become a very lucrative business. If you want to know how, read on.

Since the 1950s and Barry Bucknell's television shows *Do it yourself* and *Bucknell's House*, the British television-watching public has become more and more obsessed by DIY, and by property in general. Amidst many property-based programmes, *Property Ladder* was created to respond to the need for real information about property, offering both entertainment and hard, take-away advice. The series follows real people climbing the property ladder: buying, renovating and then selling properties to make a profit. In other words, the series shows you how to take your DIY hobby and turn it into a financially viable career.

Property Ladder – the programme – was conceived to respond to the changing aspirations of the property-buying market in recent years. People are no longer interested in cheap DIY solutions to interior design problems. They have interior designed their homes from top to bottom and now they are looking for something more – a real purpose and a point to their renovations. People from all walks of life have caught the property bug; houses and flats are flying out of the estate agents. Many people are making reasonable amounts of money, and some are making huge amounts. So how do you get to be part of the latter group? What do you have to do to make it REALLY big? How little can you really invest in a property to make the maximum profit? I hope to give you the answers.

The history of property development

While the history of property itself is of course thousands of years old, the history of property development as we recognise it today really dates back to the mid-1700s when Thomas Cubit and Joseph Nash built many of the grander terraces in London, with the direct intention of selling them on for profit. Cubit and Nash were extremely successful developers, and they made a considerable profit.

Yet it would be a long time before the concept that a house was a marketable commodity rather than simply a place in which to live caught on outside the cities. Properties were essentially built to house people. The last massive build in this country took place during the Industrial Revolution in the mid-1800s, and these are the properties that many of us live in today – the 'Victorian Terrace'.

Until around 1906 there were few planning restrictions regulating building on land outside metropolitan areas. The situation did not materially change until 1947, when the Town and Country Planning Act restricted where you could build and so reduced the supply of properties available. This meant that, for the first time, existing properties began to have a value that was more than simply how much they had cost to build.

The Industrial Revolution effectively began in Telford Iron Foundry but soon spread to the rest of the country. Demand for industrial products became so great that people from the countryside had to be persuaded to come and work in the factories. At the same time, a wave of Enclosure Acts were passed by parliament that made it legal to enclose the common land that country people had collected their food from. The country folk left their land, came to the towns for work, and many of their houses fell into disrepair and eventually fell down. Terraces of two- and three-bedroomed houses were quickly and cheaply built across the country. These houses had an outside loo and were generally either rented or came with the job. There was a basic design – and it worked. As a result terraces went up at a furious pace from Land's End to John O'Groats. There has been no serious mass building programme since. The population then was 20 million; it is now 60 million. It's not difficult to see why there's a housing shortage.

Prospects for property development today

All businesses work on the basis of supply and demand. Property development is no different. So, your first task as an aspiring property developer is to sit down and work out whether there is a demand for your product and, if so, where that demand is coming from. Demand is your bread and butter. Developing property is NOT about making a quick buck by sploshing a bit of paint around and sticking coffee beans in the oven; it's about creating a product for which there is a market.

The UK has a growing demand for property, and therefore offers more and more opportunities for the potential developer every year. The nature of those opportunities has also changed dramatically in recent years, due to lifestyle factors and technological advances. The population is made up of people who all have different passions, ideas and priorities. Not everyone's passion is DIY, and so there is a demand for a profession that provides a service to those not particularly interested in refurbishing their homes themselves and who are prepared to pay for properties that meet their requirements. Buying a newly developed house is rather like buying a new car. Many people buy a new car because they are too busy or simply not interested in dismantling the engine of their old one and putting it back together again. They just want the car to look nice and work well – they are happy to, and do, pay a premium for this luxury.

So, there is a demand for modernised properties, and all indicators suggest this demand is increasing and will continue to do so. The people who will want to buy this hassle-free home are not all of a particular type – they come from different walks of life and have a wide range of different requirements. If your developed property meets these requirements in every way then you will have a serious success on your hands.

Principles of property development

There are no *rules* as such of property development, but there are *principles* of property development. By no rules I mean that there is no single route to a tidy profit with any given property. For example, you can develop a property without totally refurbishing it – a perfectly nice two-bed house can be turned into a three-bed house by converting the loft, with the rest of the property left untouched. In some areas this may still add more value than the cost of the conversion.

The three most important principles are to appeal to a broad market, to be ruthless with your budget and to be objective with your design. Stick to these principles and you'll have less chance of getting your fingers burnt and more chance of buying that yacht in the Caribbean.

Appeal to a broad market

The key to appealing to the greatest possible number of people is not to do anything that anybody could take a dislike to, while at the same time avoiding the bland and unmemorable. I appreciate that this can be quite a tricky balance to strike, but with thorough research, and by learning from the mistakes made by people featured in the case studies in this book, you will learn how to develop and present your property in its optimal condition and have a place you'll be proud to market. You might even be a little bit jealous of the new occupants. Always focus on the difference between being a property developer and just 'doing up your house'. They are not the same thing and if you fail to understand this you're in for a rocky ride as a property developer.

Be ruthless with your budget

With property development, every penny you spend must make a difference. Be uncompromising with yourself and only invest if your calculations tell you it will be worth it. If you are renovating a property to live in yourself, different rules apply. I am not saying that there is any sin in buying a house or flat just because you want a home and to refurbish it exactly the way YOU want it, but it is not a business and as such the focus is completely different. It is about how you would like your home to look, NOT about producing a product that is easily marketable, for which there is high demand and which gives you a great lump of profit for your troubles.

Be objective

The ability to disassociate yourself from the property in question is one of the most important character traits you'll have to develop. Since primitive times, human beings have wanted to have somewhere to call home. It's not surprising, then, that it can be very difficult to cut yourself off from your own sometimes bizarre and unusually creative dreams and focus on the project in hand. Remember, you are creating a home for someone else. You don't know *exactly* who that person is, but you know their broad outline (see chapter 2, Research your market). While there may be a few people in the country who agree with you that a dark-red shagpile carpet gives the place a cosy feel, you can be sure that many more are going to have equally strong feelings against it. These people are all potential buyers, and you've lost them already.

When my boyfriend and I renovated our own home we didn't stick to any of the guidelines and principles of property development. We didn't need to, as it wasn't a business venture. A few years later, when we decided to sell, it took us a year or so to find a buyer. The house was designed by us for us and there were not that many people who were looking for a property to buy that happened to have the same personal requirements as we did. If this had been a business venture, and we had been trying to make a profit or sell it in a certain timescale, we would have been in trouble.

A personal note

Since we started developing property about seven years ago, we have (mostly) had a great time. A major contributing factor has been due to the fact that I have worked with two of my closest friends (my brother and my boyfriend), which makes being at work, rather than in the pub, not such a terrible bind!

My interest in property started when I was very young when my father (after my parents had dabbled in self-sufficiency for a few years) went back to his initial profession of designing houses. I would spend many a day holding the end of a tape measure or the ranging rod while my father carried out surveys. When I was 10 my marvellous (though slightly eccentric) father moved us into a caravan on the site where our new house was being built. For a year or so after school I would watch as our new house gradually took shape (and at weekends and holidays be encouraged to help mix cement and carry bricks). I think it was probably at this point that my brother and I realised that building was so in our bones that we were unlikely to spend much of our lives not up to our ears in mud and concrete, and we decided we might as well go with the flow. Having dropped at least thirty 1p pieces into the cavity wall as it was being built, convinced that one day in the future an archaeologist would thank me for it, I began to understand that a new house was a piece of history of the future. A home is one of humanity's most treasured possessions – this seemed a good enough reason for me to stick with it.

When I was in my early twenties, I thought seriously, with five friends, about developing a property. Three of us – my brother, my boyfriend and myself – decided to go ahead. Our first property was a split-level ground and basement flat. We fitted it with a new kitchen, retiled the bathroom and fitted new taps, redecorated throughout, landscaped the garden, and sorted out the exterior – all in about 14 days, working through the days and most of the nights (eating a lot of take-away food and drinking a lot of take-away beer!). I can't pretend it wasn't hard work, because it certainly was, but we sold the property pretty quickly and made a very good profit. After that we were off. A couple of years later we decided to buy properties to retain, and this signalled the beginning of our investment company.

I have never underestimated how much easier it is to develop property with other like-minded people than on your own. Not only do I LIKE doing the work, I also LIKE the people I do it with; so in effect I am being paid to do what I like doing. If you are lucky enough to be in a similar situation then the rewards you can reap from property development will be considerably enhanced.

Is property development for you?

You don't have to have a lot of money to start in property development, it is all a question of attitude, determination and how much you really want to succeed.

To be a property developer you must display the following character traits – good organisational skills, dedication and commitment. To be a very successful property developer, however, rather than one who dips their toes in property before deciding it's all too much like hard work, you must have a genuine interest in and love of all types, shapes, sizes and features of buildings, plus an astute business head and a great deal of energy. You must have a deep-rooted fascination with not only the buildings themselves but with how and why people live in them in the way that they do. Developing can be a great job and it is very enjoyable to create something you are proud of but it is not a licence to print money any more than any other job.

Have you got what it takes?

This questionnaire is designed to help you discover whether you are cut out for property development. Be strict with yourself and answer all the questions truthfully.

1 When you walk past an estate agent's window do you find yourself magnetically drawn to the photographs?

2 When you go to someone else's home do you take them up on the offer of having a good look around?

3 Would you pick up *Homes and Gardens* before *OK!* magazine in the dentist's waiting room?

4 Are you able to set yourself a precise spending limit and not go over it when you go on holiday?

5 When you go to a car boot sale do you haggle over a high price rather than go red and walk away?

6 When friends ask you to give them a hand re-landscaping their garden for the weekend do you feel excited about getting down to some hard but creative work or do you invent a terrible incapacitating illness?

7 Look back through your diary for the last three months and see what you have done in the evenings and weekends – would you have been prepared to miss most of these events?

8 Are you happy for your 12-year-old niece to show you an easier way to build your flat-packed table than the way you were doing it?

9 Would you fix a dripping tap as soon as you discovered it or would you wait several months?

10 Would you work out how to change a washer and do it yourself rather than phone a plumber?

11 When a crisis happens are you able to think of a logical way out or do you reach for the gin?

If you can honestly answer yes to the all above questions then you might well have the right sort of character to succeed in property development. The sacrifices you will have to make will be considerable.

What do you want to achieve?

If you're confident that you have the right character to make it as a property developer, the next question you need to ask yourself is whether you're after hard work and quick gain or hard work and long-term gain. In other words, whether you want to concentrate on selling properties or on renting properties.

We had already been running our development company and concentrating on buying properties to sell on for a couple of years before we decided to get into the rather different business of buying properties to let. From my experience in these two areas, I must stress how important it is that you recognise that selling and renting are two very different forms of property development. They have different criteria, different tax implications, different priorities. I could not honestly say that I believe one to be easier or better than the other. But you need to decide very early on the direction you want to take.

Selling

Do you want to be able to access your profit soon after completing the building works on your development? If so, you should be looking at finding, developing and selling a property.

Selling the property will provide you with a lump of cash that you can use in a number of ways:

• to replace your salary if you decide to give up work and develop property as a full-time career

• to lower the amount of the loan you need to take out on your next development

• to buy a bigger property and move up the property ladder

• to buy two smaller properties to develop

• to spend on a holiday, new car, etc.

Don't forget your profit is gross and so will be liable to tax.

Renting

Are you looking at developing a property and keeping it as a long-term investment? If so, you need to look at renting.

We all know that having some form of long-term investment to provide us with an income in our old age is even more important today than it was in years gone by. National pensions may not even exist by the time many of us reach retirement age and so we need to develop other sources of income to provide for our security in later life. There are various stock market investments you can use to provide you with an

There is a lot more to renting than receiving a direct debit into your bank account every month

alternative pension vehicle. Some of these funds may themselves invest in property while others may invest in various different businesses. Developing a property yourself to rent out and keep as a long-term investment CAN provide this pension alternative – when the mortgage is paid off the rental income provides you with something to live on in retirement – but will require you to do with a lot of work and can be a great deal of hassle. There is a lot more to renting than receiving a direct debit into your bank account every month, and it will be your responsibility to make sure that the property arrangement provides you with the income you are after. The good news is that with renting you are in control – perfect for those of us who like the excitement and uncertainty of being an employer, rather than the relative security of being an employee. See pages 135 to 146 for more on renting.

What this book will tell you

The aim of this book is to show you how to make money from property. It is not an interior decorating book. Neither is it a DIY book, though both these areas will be touched on as they impact on your ability to achieve a successful sale. Above all, the focus is on how to produce the product that your particular market wants and to lay the foundations for a profitable business. What is apparent, especially from the feedback from viewers, is that there is a desperate need for hard facts and information to guide people who are either buying a home or interested in taking their first steps in a career in property development. With this book (which is mainly being written due to the number of requests from viewers of the programme), I hope to pass on the benefit of my experience and clear a path for you through the sometimes confusing and occasionally daunting world of property refurbishment and development.

1

RESEARCH YOUR MARKET

Understanding who you are targeting really is the key to the entire success of your development project. Before you do any work at all, you need to establish who is going to buy your property once it is beautifully refurbished. Who is going to give you all this money that you think you deserve? This chapter will help you decide on both your market and your area.

Deciding on your market

The market for buying or renting properties can generally be split into the following categories. Their relative importance will vary depending on the area. To work out which sector of the market you should be targeting your property towards study the market descriptions below. You should also check out the local amenities to see who the shops and services are geared to and bear this in mind to help you identify your market.

Students

This market wants to pay low rent and needs to be near a quick and easy transport link. Students are happy to share, and don't expect high-quality fittings. This market is the ideal rental market. Look out for cheap properties – large flats, flats above shops, big houses with lots of bedrooms – in cheap areas near a university or college, or at least near to transport links that will take students quickly to their place of study. There will always be students who want cheap, easy accommodation. You should be aware that students are unlikely to want to pay rent during the holidays (which are long) and so the property may lie empty for up to 15 weeks of the year. However, you may be able to organise short lets, perhaps to students attending a summer school, or even to professionals on work placements, provided the quality of the accommodation is sufficiently high.

Students normally have come straight from living at home, and so have not been responsible for a property before. They are invariably less aware of how to maintain a property (and probably less 'house-proud' than professional renters) so you will need to check the property regularly and accept that you are likely to have to redecorate it fairly often. Don't provide students with anything that needs constant attention (like a beach-block worktop that needs oiling regularly) as they probably won't do it and you will simply end up having to replace it.

First-time buyers/young professionals (early-to-mid 20s)

Think about those graduates who have just started their professional careers. They're eager to step onto the first rung of the property ladder and are sick of skuzzy living quarters and of living with lots of people with little or no reception space. They have certain basic requirements – they want functional, spacious accommodation in reasonable areas – but they cannot yet afford luxuries. Look for good two/three-bedroomed flats (with every bedroom large enough to accommodate at least a small double bed) in up-and-coming areas and with good transport links.

For people in this market, this is probably the first time they have tried to cook something other than spaghetti bolognaise, so you'll need to provide a practical, inspiring kitchen but you won't need to splash out on lots of units as these buyers will not have as many possessions as older professionals or families who've had years to

There will always be students who want cheap, easy accommodation

accumulate them. This is a great market to sell to as buyers generally do not have a property to sell themselves and so the purchase should be able to go through very quickly. The building needs to be very sound as they are unlikely to have much of a deposit and so will be buying the property mostly with a mortgage. They don't have the funds to deal with a retention from the mortgage company or to come up with a load of cash to put towards external maintenance.

Young professionals also represent a good rental market, particularly in large cities. They often opt to share while saving for a deposit to buy their own property and in some parts of the country house prices may simply be too high for them to contemplate buying. The same rules apply as for the student rental sector, but with higher-quality fittings and finishes.

Older professionals (late 20s, early 30s)

These are probably second-time buyers who have worked for several years, increased their disposable income and are moving on. This market expects more in terms of design and quality of fittings. Having had the experience of living in their own homes for a few years they know exactly what they want and will demand fairly high standards. Entertaining space is essential – kitchen/breakfast rooms rather than galley kitchens are a key selling feature with this group. They want a sophisticated hot water system with powerful showers (see pages 109 to 110) and lots of bathrooms (in a perfect world you would have one bathroom per bedroom, but I would always recommend a minimum bedroom to bathroom ratio of 3:1. With this market you can to a certain extent unleash your talent for cutting-edge design. Keep abreast of what the latest fashions are in materials, kitchen design, flooring and colours by visiting interiors shops and looking at the latest magazines and catalogues. This will help you fully understand this particular market.

Young couples

Young couples setting up home and perhaps hoping for or with their first baby are an important sector of the market. They usually prefer to buy houses to flats and the garden is a high priority. This is probably the first home the couple has bought together and often they may be selling two flats in order to buy a house. So now you have two people to please.

The irritating cliché that women are mainly interested in the kitchen is, I'm afraid, one I don't hold to. However, the kitchen IS important to many families in general. If a new baby is pretty much putting an end to evenings out, eating will be done primarily at home, with the kitchen the area in which the family will tend to congregate. A galley kitchen is unlikely to appeal to this market. Make sure the property is a comfortable one – families with young children may prefer carpets to wooden floors – and that it is, above all, a 'home'. Choose a fairly well-established area near local schools, shops and other amenities.

Growing families

With this market the kids are growing up, beginning to invite friends round and therefore demanding more privacy. The family needs more space and can now afford more conveniences and luxuries. Large houses, with sufficiently large gardens, and with living spaces ideally separated out, will therefore always be in demand. Most large families find that top-end design and open-plan living simply doesn't make for staying sane and the result is that everything ends up being just one big mess. Plenty of storage is needed, a garden is essential and off-street parking highly desirable. Again, it is good to be near facilities, though transport does not need to be on the doorstep and a quiet street will in fact add points to the property.

Downsizing households

Older people often find that the home that once seemed simply adequate starts to grow. This can be for a number of reasons: the children have left home; they are entertaining less; they simply don't have the energy to run a large house any longer; or they are looking to release some of the capital from their home in order to fully enjoy their retirement. Whatever the reason, the requirements of this market are very clear: a smaller home is needed, where everything works – the dining area needs to be in or near the kitchen, the windows and doors need to be easy to lock and unlock, etc. – and which is easy to maintain. Bungalows are popular with this market, and low-maintenance (though pretty) gardens are essential. Stick to practical and simple design and use furnishings and materials that create a comfortable and cosy feel for the interior.

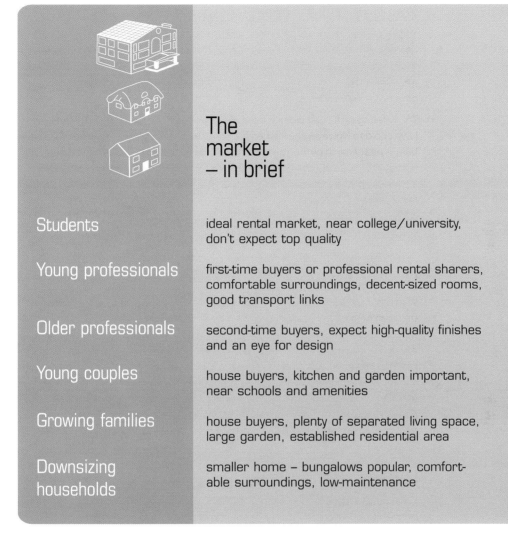

The market – in brief

Students
ideal rental market, near college/university, don't expect top quality

Young professionals
first-time buyers or professional rental sharers, comfortable surroundings, decent-sized rooms, good transport links

Older professionals
second-time buyers, expect high-quality finishes and an eye for design

Young couples
house buyers, kitchen and garden important, near schools and amenities

Growing families
house buyers, plenty of separated living space, large garden, established residential area

Downsizing households
smaller home – bungalows popular, comfortable surroundings, low-maintenance

The key is to appeal to as many of these market categories as possible. The greater the number of different groups interested the more likely you'll be to get the sale at the price you want. The ideal situation is to have two or more interested buyers – you have a greater chance of achieving your asking price and getting a speedy sale. Whoever wants to buy the property will move more quickly if they know other purchasers are snapping at their heels. As a developer, one of the greatest feelings is to have a potential purchaser who has lost out on one of your properties ask if you have any other similar developments coming up. Then you know you have produced the right product.

Deciding on an area

It is important to realise that property developers can make money in ANY kind of area. The principle being that as long as you buy your property for the right price, aim for the right market, renovate accordingly, spend the right amount of money and sell it for more than it has cost you, you will make a profit. This principle will work in most places, in most countries of the world.

When you're starting out, you're probably best advised to focus on an area you know at least something about. This means you'll have knowledge about the area that you just cannot pick up on simply by walking around. You might also have useful information about how the area has changed in recent years, and how it might potentially change in the near future.

Once you start researching your area, you will quickly get an idea of the sort of people that are being attracted to it, and how house prices are affected by this. The general rule is that the better the services and transport links, the stronger property prices will be. These areas are generally very well established and house prices are likely to always be reasonably stable.

Get ahead

Ask around to see if any major investment is planned into any local schools or if there is a reorganisation in the pipeline that is likely to improve a particular school. As word gets out, more and more people will want to live in the area, thus pushing up the demand for properties (the greater the number of people that want something the more valuable that thing becomes).

Spotting an established area – the cappuccino test!

As a general rule, people with a fair amount of disposable income will live in the established areas. By 'a fair amount' I mean that, on top of general living expenses, this market has money to burn.

They will spend their spare money on the general upkeep of their properties, several holidays a year, plenty of meals out, etc. Telltale signs of an established area include attractive front gardens, well cared-for exteriors and litter-free pavements. The people who make up this market are usually fairly young, tend to be single, and demand places in which to spend their extra cash, so look out for consumer-led businesses

such as swanky restaurants, trendy bars and cafes, lots of estate agents, both adult
and children's boutique shops and the ultimate established-area give-aways, a Pizza
Express and a cappuccino bar.

Checklist – know your area

Visit estate agents in the area and pick up sets of details ☐

Get a feel for the range of housing stock available in the area
– are there lots of conversions, modern developments, etc? ☐

Compare prices of similar properties in different streets and if they differ
ask around as to why this is ☐

Look up the school league tables and work out which schools
(both primary and secondary) are producing the best results ☐

Find out where local shopping facilities are and check out
the types of shops and services on offer ☐

Work out the route on public transport from any property
you are considering to key areas of employment ☐

Work out the journey time for this route ☐

Check out the route to motorways or the main train stations;
this is particularly important for properties in commuter belts ☐

See what types of cars are parked outside the homes ☐

 Rural areas

The property market in the countryside tends to move a bit more slowly than in
urban areas, especially when larger properties are involved. This is partly due to the
fact that the purchaser is often in a chain. Transport is not so important in the
countryside – it is so limited that people don't expect it, and they tend to drive to get
where they want. However, a good local rail link to a city will certainly add value. Good
local amenities i.e. a busy local town or village and, of course, good schools are all
things to look out for.

Up-and-coming areas

As the demand for convenience living has increased, property prices in many established areas have shot through the roof, rendering it almost impossible for those not yet on the property ladder to be able to afford to buy in these areas. Britain has a culture, unlike many other European countries, where it is considered relatively normal to own rather than rent your home. Children in Britain traditionally leave the family home earlier than many of their European counterparts and this, coupled with recent low interest rates and the increase in single-parent families, has created increased demand and contributed to this purchasing frenzy. As a result, demand for good-quality, affordable housing has driven buyers further and further afield. And it is this demand that is behind the phenomenon of the up-and-coming area.

Guessing where are the next up-and-coming areas always invites a lot of speculation. The truth is that if anyone actually knew which they were, then he or she would be very rich. Huge investment into an area can bring property prices up quickly but this is by no means automatic. A lot of money came in to the Docklands area of London, for example, in the late 1980s/early 1990s, but the people failed to follow, sending many very wealthy investors back to the drawing board. This can be partly attributed to the delay in transport improvements in the area, which initially failed to keep pace with the booming business activity. When these transport improvements did come, they had a significant effect on the area and now it has very much up and come.

Beat the competition	Go for a location that is already popular and then look for properties which are nearby. Look for the next stop down on the underground, or the next stop on the bus route. Look out for an area where there is a great deal of investment planned (i.e. a new business park being built) or where there are new transport links in the pipeline.

Despite this uncertainty, it is often true that the next area to come up is likely to be next door to an already popular area. Many buyers will be prepared to compromise on their ideal location in order to buy a larger property adjacent to the area in which they really want to live. This is called the ripple effect.

With all areas, the golden rule is RESEARCH, RESEARCH and RESEARCH AGAIN. Do not be tempted to buy a lighthouse off John O' Groats to develop just because it looks like a film set – unless of course you are confident (through your research) not only of what you are going to do with it but also that there is a market for the end product. Properties near a railway line, on a main road, above a shop, or near an electricity pylon are generally cheaper, as these locations can make buyers a bit nervous. This does not necessarily mean you should not develop such properties, however. Remember, EVERY property is a good deal at the right price – you will get less for it when you sell it but you should have paid less money for it in the first place, so your profit is still safe.

Buying in a rising market – a word of warning

Trading or speculating on the property market is not the same thing as property developing. It simply means buying properties and either waiting for the market to change in some way or selling the property to someone who will pay more for it than you did in the state in which you bought it. This is effectively the same as if you were a broker trading in the stock market – brokers are not doing anything to actually add value to the shares, they are gambling on outside forces that are driving the prices up or down. While a rising market may seem like an exciting way of gaining lottery-type amounts of money for doing almost nothing, it is important to be realistic about what is actually happening. A slow and steady growth in property prices undoubtedly benefits everyone but a very buoyant market where property prices rise dramatically over a short time-period carries with it the danger of unsustainable growth and the knock-on effect of the market becoming overheated and either levelling off or actually dropping (as happened in the 1980s). Either way, there is little that you can actually do to affect the market (unless you have the buying power of an oil tycoon). If you are making profit on a property due to the rising market rather than actually adding value by changes you make to the property yourself, then you might as well buy a newly modernised home that someone else has sweated blood over and enjoy living there until it is time to sell.

Your profit should always be calculated on the basis of the value of the property on the day you purchased it. This way, if the market rises, so well and good, but if it does drop it will still have a long way to go before you actually make no profit at all. Don't forget that as prices go up, unless you are planning on jacking it all in and spending your capital backpacking around the world (quite tempting at times) you will have to spend more on the next property you buy so you don't actually gain that much in the grand scheme of things. The only one to really gain from a rising market is the Chancellor of the Exchequer, as the more properties cost the more stamp duty is due.

Buying in a rising market

Simon and Caitlin realised it was worth spending some of their budget on tidying up the front of the house. They bought a new front door to brighten things up, which increased the property's appeal for potential buyers.

Simon and Caitlin Eisenmann are a young couple living in Norwich. Unable to find their dream house, they decided to sell their existing property and move into rented accommodation so that they could keep looking and move fast once they saw the perfect house. As the months went by without anything suitable coming up they grew increasingly aware that the market was rising fast and that the capital they'd made from the sale of their previous house was sitting there and not really working for them. They also began to realise their dream house was actually their rental home (and their landlord did agree to sell them the house), but they were £7,000 short of the asking price. They decided to buy a small, unmodernised property, renovate it and sell it on in the hope of making the £7,000 they needed to buy the property they were renting.

The Budget   £

Property bought for	£45,000
Projected cost of works	£7,000 max
Projected sale price	£59,000
Gross profit required to buy rented property	£7,000

What they bought

Simon and Caitlin decided to buy a small, walk-in terraced property on a busy main road in an up-and-coming part of north Norwich. The ground floor of the property had a main living room at the front of the house, with a second reception room directly behind it, and the kitchen at the back of the house. To the rear was a 20-ft garden. The stairs separated the two downstairs reception rooms, running parallel with the road. On the first floor there was a double bedroom above each of the reception rooms. The only bathroom was above the kitchen, accessed only via the rear bedroom.

The plan

The house needed a complete refurbishment. Simon and Caitlin planned to install central heating and have a damp proof course fitted. They also planned to replace the flat roof above the kitchen and have the whole house rewired and replumbed.

My advice

TARGET THE BROADEST MARKET. I was mainly concerned that the only bathroom for the whole house was accessible solely through the second bedroom, because this would greatly limit their market. The only people interested in the property would be single people, or couples, perhaps with small children. The property would not appeal to professional sharers because anyone sleeping in the front bedroom would have to go through the back bedroom each time they wanted to use the bathroom. I suggested they build an upstairs corridor along the side wall of the house to give both bedrooms private access to the bathroom. All Simon and Caitlin had to do to achieve this was knock a doorway into the back of the cupboard from the front bedroom, steal some space from bedroom number two and build a stud wall through to the bathroom. Then they would simply create another doorway from bedroom two into the new corridor. This whole service would have only cost them another £800. I had no doubt it would have added at least another £4,000 onto the asking price.

RESTORE ORIGINAL FEATURES. I advised Simon and Caitlin to put back as many of the Victorian features as possible into the house in order to attain their maximum asking price. Buyers in Norwich, in their particular market, would expect Victorian fireplaces, cornices, picture rails and door handles in a period property.

Simon and Caitlin created an attractive and manageable family garden, with an outside entertaining space in the form of a gazebo with table and chairs.

Simon and Caitlin rejected my corridor idea. They'd lived in a house with this layout once and hadn't found the bathroom access a problem, so couldn't understand why it might be an issue for others. Two out of three local estate agents confirmed that if they had in fact gone for the corridor idea it would have increased the value of their property by at least another £4,000 (a further £3,200 profit!). They did eventually finish their development, but went way over schedule (21 weeks instead of 12) and way over budget (£13,062 instead of £7,000). However, they did do a reasonable job and put a lot of effort into the presentation of the property.

Their poor budgeting and planning could have cost them dearly. But Simon and Caitlin got lucky. In the five months they spent working on the house the property market in Norwich rose dramatically. This masked the fact that they had effectively lost time and money through delays of their own making. You should never rely on a rising market to make your money from developing. The market can change from one day to the next and there is no guarantee that a dramatic rise will not be followed by an equally dramatic fall. And besides, in a rising market the next property you'll want to buy is likely to have also increased in price, so any profit you think you have made is effectively swallowed up in your next purchase.

Final sums

Property bought for	£45,000
Final cost of works:	
Modernising and kitchen	£5,400
Materials, fireplace and doors	£1,920
Extra labour	£2,450
Mortgage repayments	£1,616
Professional fees	£1,676
Total	**£13,062**
Target selling price (given the rise in the market)	£71,950
Target gross profit	**£13,888 (24%)**

Simon and Caitlin got three valuations, at £69,995, £71,950 and £74,950. Sensibly, they decided not to go for the top price. Accepting a midway valuation means you should attract a number of serious offers. They accepted an offer from a young couple at the full asking price. So, their hard work did pay off and earned them a

Simon and Caitlin bought their kitchen for under £1,000. They focussed on accessories, rather than overspending on carcasses and units, as this was right for their market.

handsome profit of £13,888. Nevertheless, this did have a lot to do with the rise in property prices in the Norwich market – they could have made the same or a very similar amount of money by purchasing an already modernised house and spending the 21 weeks with their feet up before selling it again. **(2001)**

Being realistic about your commitments

To keep costs down, Simon and Caitlin decided to do most of the work themselves, a tough challenge, considering they had to finish the project in just 12 weeks. Like many people renovating their first property, Simon and Caitlin underestimated the commitment needed. After a period of time, they began to struggle. Both had full-time jobs and were finding it hard to project manage, let alone get the actual work done. Eventually I persuaded them to get in professional builders, decorators and gardeners. Being realistic about the amount of time and commitment required is crucially important when developing property. If you know you're not prepared to sacrifice your Saturday-morning lie-in, or if you have lots of social commitments, then budget for the professionals to come in and do the work instead.

Where are they now?

Simon and Caitlin decided not to use their profit to buy their rented accommodation and instead bought a different house in a new trendy development on the outskirts of Norwich. Soon after, they also invested in a terraced property in Lowestoft, Suffolk and even bought a second house containing three separate, self-contained flats. They are renting out all these properties and even after tax making a healthy profit. **(2002)**

2
GETTING ORGANISED

So you've decided that you really want to do this, you're prepared to make the necessary sacrifices, you've identified your market and you've decided on your area. Now is the time to start making it all happen. This chapter looks at finding a property, finding the money and working out a realistic budget.

Finding a property

The range of sources of property for sale has increased quite dramatically in recent years. The high-street estate agent will still be your main port of call, but you should keep an open mind with regard to alternatives, such as private sales, buying off the plan and auctions.

The right deal

Your first step is to contact several estate agents in the area in which you are hoping to buy. Explain clearly what you are looking for and register your details with them. Ring the agents periodically to check that they haven't forgotten you and never be late for appointments unless absolutely unavoidable. If you really can't make an appointment, give plenty of notice – nobody likes to be stood up, it's just plain rude. As with all working relationships a good rapport with your agent is essential. The agent is the one most familiar with the local market and area and you need to make sure he or she is always on your side. See pages 132 to 134 for more tips on working with estate agents.

When you see the property you want do not be tempted to dilly dally – put an offer in as soon as possible. If you go away to think about it for too long it just might have sold by the time you come back with an offer, so trust your instincts. If your offer is accepted instruct your solicitor immediately and ask your mortgage company to instruct their valuer. This is not the time for the laid-back approach – you are making the first step towards your profit!

Auctions

Property auctions are another way you can purchase a property. The process is fast and furious and there can be pitfalls – I would approach them with caution if it is your first development. If you are very lucky and no-one else at the auction really wants the property then it is possible to pick up a bargain. However, you must be prepared for the fact that you can waste a great deal of time looking at properties, working out budgets and poring over the paperwork only to find that when it comes to the auction you don't even get a chance to put your hand up before it has gone over the price you were prepared to pay.

The golden rule is to set your top limit and STICK TO IT. Do not be tempted to treat an auction as a monopoly game just because it feels as if that's what everyone else is doing. Remember, you are bidding in thousands of pounds not hundreds – it's a lot of money! Be aware that vendors may well put a property up for auction if there are complications. Auctioning the property achieves a quick sale for what could otherwise take a very long time. It is therefore vital to understand ALL of the paperwork relevant to the property and be absolutely sure of what you are doing before you go ahead and buy via auction. There are property auctions all over the country. Your local paper or the Internet will tell you which companies are local to you.

Buying off the plan

This means that you buy a property before it's built or developed and is a popular method of bankrolling with large developments – the deposit the developer takes from you before they have started work shows their financier that they have a guaranteed sale when they have finished the property, and so helps their cash flow. For this they will be happy to reduce the price of the property from what it is likely to be worth when it is actually built. Generally speaking, therefore, the property will be worth more when you move into it than when you put down your deposit. It is really a form of financing large developments in a cooperative way. If all goes well this is a good form of property investment. If it doesn't – the property market drops while it is being built – you are still liable to complete on the purchase at the same price. Make sure you check the contract front to back, back to front and sideways, and try to find out about other recent projects by the same development company.

The Internet

The Internet is no longer tomorrow's technology, it is today's – face it and get surfing! There are some great sites where sellers advertise their properties privately. They will probably put photographs of the property on the website – this is a good starting point but nothing more. To get any sort of real feel for the property you must visit in person. Most estate agents and auction houses will have their own websites, some providing 'virtual tours' of properties for sale, and you should check these regularly. Agents' websites also offer a quick and easy way of comparing prices without having to leave the house. See page 171 for useful property website addresses.

Private sales

This may well be a good way of finding a property although you risk wasting a lot of time as vendors are prone to colour their description of the property they are selling and describe it in a totally unrealistic way over the phone. It also means that you are negotiating directly with the vendor. Of course, they avoid paying an agent's commission but you have no middle man to call on should difficulties arise. Make sure that you are clear from the start what you expect to be included in the sale and always ensure you both confirm in writing anything you agree verbally.

Local papers

These can be a great way to get a real feel for the market and for which areas and types of property different agents tend to specialise in. Papers will carry details of private sales and auctions too. I would advise you look carefully at the property section for several weeks before buying a property – that way you can be relatively confident of not only catching the right property when it comes up but also that the sale price you are hoping for is not too way off the mark.

The importance of research

Dan and Rowena bought a standard semi-detached house to develop in Coventry. They believed the property market in the city was about to take off.

Dan and Rowena are two people with dreams. They have been together for just over a year, after meeting through work. Dan lives with his parents and works in London, while Rowena lives and works in Coventry with her teenage son, Chris. Dan was very keen to get onto the property ladder, but was unable to afford the London prices, so it seemed an ideal opportunity to look for a property to develop in Coventry.

The Budget   £

Property bought for	£54,000
Projected cost of works	£11,000
Projected sale price	£75,000
Projected gross profit	£10,000 (15.4% – not bad for an initial outlay of £1,000!)

Dan only had £1,000 in savings, yet with this small amount of capital, and a huge helping hand from the bank, Dan and Rowena managed to secure the property they wanted. In fact, they took out a 98% mortgage and an unsecured loan to bring their borrowing up to 120% of the value of the property. This is never something I would advocate – the risks involved are high and if the market turns or you make the wrong decision, you stand to lose an awful lot. Having said that, I was always convinced that Dan and Rowena would do well because 1) they had total commitment to and enthusiasm for the project 2) they put a huge amount of time and effort into their research 3) they were prepared to keep an open mind and listen to my advice (something that people on the show don't generally do!).

What they bought

Dan and Rowena might not have had a lot of money with which to start developing, but what they lacked in pennies they made up for with ingenuity. They gave themselves plenty of time to thoroughly research the area. They learnt that in Birmingham – the focus of much recent regeneration – house prices had risen quite considerably, while in nearby Coventry prices were still relatively low. Property patterns would typically dictate that Coventry would be one of the next areas to take off and attract many first-time buyers, especially young families. Dan and Rowena therefore decided (correctly) to target this market. They checked the school league tables for Coventry on the Internet and worked out the catchment areas of the top schools. Then they searched for a property which matched the requirements of a young family, i.e. a house, with two or more bedrooms, good-sized reception rooms, a good-sized kitchen, a large bathroom and a decent-sized garden – and on or close to a popular street.

The property they bought had a sitting room to the right as you walked through the front door, a large kitchen at the back of the house, a loo accessed from outside, which stole space from the kitchen, and a 130-ft garden. Upstairs there were three bedrooms, two of which could have been considered a good size. There was also a very small bathroom.

Dan and Rowena installed a relatively contemporary kitchen, but made sure it was of a design that would appeal to a broad market.

The plan

Dan and Rowena had two major issues to deal with in this property.

1. The kitchen space. They could see that the outside loo would not be attractive to today's buyers. They initially decided to keep the loo and access it from inside the kitchen, which provided a downstairs cloakroom. They were hoping that the two loos would be seen as a bonus by the family market they were targeting and therefore increase the property's value. They also wanted to knock out the chimneybreast in the kitchen, which they hoped would enhance the feeling of space.

2. The proportions of the house. The house felt very small, especially the bathroom. Dan and Rowena needed to somehow create the impression of space, but without knocking down any walls and keeping to a very tight budget.

If a bedroom is large enough to be described as a double room, then it's best to actually put in a double bed, so that the buyer can see how the room could be used.

Dan and Rowena effectively staged the living room with carefully selected furniture and accessories to suggest to buyers how they might actually live in the house.

My advice

CREATE THE RIGHT KITCHEN FOR THE PROPERTY. I advised them to knock out the outside loo and to incorporate the space into the kitchen. This would add more value than an extra loo would as families really appreciate kitchens large enough to house a table at which they can all eat. I also advised them to leave the chimneybreast in place (removing it would have been very expensive) and instead make a design feature of it by arranging the kitchen units around the far end of the kitchen only. This was the right advice for Dan and Rowena because a) they were on a limited budget and b) a kitchen/breakfast room was essential for their target market.

GET THE PROPORTIONS RIGHT. The property did feel small but as I explained, it wasn't the size of their property that was a problem, but the size of the fixtures and furnishings – by far the preferable of the two dilemmas! This was especially apparent in the bathroom – the bath, sink and loo were all too big for the room, which made it feel tiny. They were able to rectify this by removing the original fixtures and replacing them with smaller units that were in proportion to the room. They also rehung the door so that it opened against the wall, thus opening up the entire room.

Dan and Rowena got off to the right start by finding out as much as possible about the area, reading all the local papers and looking at property they knew they weren't interested in – just to learn as much as they could before they made that first dramatic step of buying. Dan had almost no DIY skills when he started, but he persevered and was continually trying to learn about building and renovating. They got quote after quote, asked question after question and double-checked all information. Rowena was almost fanatical about getting the best deal and keeping costs down. In the end, their research even led them to source some products from abroad.

The couple were very lucky. Due to the rising market in Coventry the valuations came in higher than they were expecting at £82,500, £83,000 and £85,000. They decided to

Dan and Rowena turned what appeared to be a small, cluttered bathroom into a bright spacious one by using smaller fittings that were more in proportion to the room. The new bathroom offered plenty of space for any family.

put the house on the market at the top valuation and were offered the full asking price within one day, making them a gross profit of £13,891.

Final sums

Property bought for	£54,000
Final cost of works:	
Windows	£2,137
Modernisation	£4,830
Kitchen and bathroom	£3,133
Contractors	£1,755
Finishing touches	£1,194
Professional fees	£4,060
Total	**£17,129**
Target selling price	£75,000
Target gross profit	**£3,871 (5.4%)**

Despite the problems they faced, Dan and Rowena managed to keep the work on schedule and the end product looked fantastic, particularly the kitchen. Their superb organisation and research, plus Dan's willingness to learn anything and everything about DIY, made for a virtually problem-free development. However, despite all their hard budgeting, the final cost of works was more than £6,000 over their original budget – £17,129 as opposed to the projected £11,000. Most of this was because they failed to include all their buying and professional fees and selling costs. It ALWAYS pays to be realistic about your budget. **(2002)**

The importance of a contingency

Despite doing a fantastic job on the development, Dan and Rowena did fall down in one crucial area. They had no contingency. A contingency fund (which should be 10% of your overall budget) is paramount when developing a property. Something will always go wrong and if you can't sort it out and stay in budget then you'll be stuck. Once the project had started Dan and Rowena realised there was a chance the Artexed ceiling in the living room and kitchen would need to be removed professionally (all pre 1978 Artex contains asbestos). Luckily, investigations revealed no trace of asbestos. Then another problem came along. Halfway into the project Dan and Rowena were told there was a good chance they would both be made redundant, with only a month's notice. The 120% mortgage suddenly looked like a huge liability, though Dan did have insurance to cover the loan. Nevertheless, in the absence of a contingency their development dream could easily have been in tatters. Luckily, after a month-and-a-half of nail-biting worry, Dan and Rowena's old jobs were reinstated. But I hardly need to say that you cannot rely on this sort of luck!

Where are they now?

Dan and Rowena decided to spend some of their profit on a well-earned holiday, after which they hope to look for another property to develop. **(2002)**

Finding the money

If you're starting out in property development, it's a pretty safe bet you'll need to take out a mortgage to buy your first property. This book is not the place to find out about the seemingly endless different types of borrowing on offer, which, in any case, can change almost on a daily basis. However, there are broad rules that you need to be aware of, and types of mortgage specifically geared to property development.

Getting your mortgage in place

In recent years lending institutions have been falling over themselves to lend you money (even up to 120% of the value of the property, as we discovered in one of the programmes). Yet if you think that this state of affairs is going to make property development a breeze, think again. Your BUDGET is what counts. You may be able to borrow more money but this does not mean that your circumstances have changed.

There are various ways to get your mortgage in place. I would recommend speaking to an independent mortgage advisor. Alternatively, talk to your bank or building society, and study magazines and newspaper financial sections that advertise the latest deals. Some of the most useful publications are *What Mortgage?* magazine, *Mortgage Magazine*, *Money Observer* and *Moneywise*. This is an area in which comprehensive research early on in the process will really pay off. Start your research before you start looking for your property – you don't want to be held up or, even worse, have the deal fall through because you didn't get their finance in place. Don't forget that when your mortgage broker quotes you the typical monthly repayments these are exclusive of insurances and water, gas, electricity, telephone and council tax fees. Check the small print and hunt around to avoid unpleasant surprises.

Types of mortgage

There are effectively two types of mortgage – repayment mortgages and interest-only. A repayment mortgage means you repay part of the loan, together with interest on the loan, on a monthly basis. An interest-only mortgage means you pay the interest on the loan each month, but the amount of the outstanding loan remains the same. With an interest-only mortgage it is common to have a separate savings vehicle so that at the end of your mortgage term you have a lump sum with which to pay off the original loan. These separate savings are often investments either in the form of an endowment, ISA (Individual Savings Account) or pension mortgage, which are effectively stock market investments. Alternatively, you might opt for a flexible interest-only mortgage. This means that you pay the interest monthly but can repay lump sums periodically to reduce your borrowing in chunks. Also, there is the one-account mortgage, which means all your savings and borrowings are with the same institution and you can pay in and withdraw at your convenience, paying interest only on the amount outstanding at any particular time.

Getting a mortgage on a second property

If you're not living in the property you are developing and not renting or living with family, you'll probably already have one mortgage. You will therefore need to take out a second mortgage in order to buy the property you intend to develop. If you are in this position it is essential that you discuss your financial circumstances with an independent mortgage advisor, who will know all the mortgage deals available. Make sure you are entirely honest with your advisor about your intentions for the second property so that they can arrange the right mortgage to fit your requirements.

Buy-to-let

The term 'buy-to-let' was created by lending institutions to classify residential properties bought with the sole intention of letting out.

An individual taking out a buy-to-let mortgage may have their own income as well as that of the rental income taken into consideration by the mortgage provider and will be able to borrow money at similar rates to those offered to a normal homeowner. At times less volatile than many other forms of investment, a buy-to-let can offer an attractive home for your savings. You'll get an annual return and also hopefully a means of enjoying long-term capital growth. (The concern over what sort of pensions will be available by the time younger members of the population reach retirement age has led people to consider buy-to-let as an investment alternative.) A word of caution, however: approach all mortgages that have a 'low starter' element with your eyes open, and think carefully about what will actually happen when the low starter bit runs out.

Don't forget that with buy-to-let mortgages you will need to have enough money to pay for ground rent and service charges as well if it is a leasehold property. Mortgage companies generally require your income from renting the property to be 125 to 140% of the amount of the monthly repayment. However, if all does go according to plan and you buy the right property at the right price, get reliable tenants and are realistic about the effort involved, buy-to-let can provide you with both a handy income as well as a comforting alternative pension plan.

Finding a good accountant

This is almost as important as finding a good solicitor (see page 132). Your accountant must understand not only your entire financial position but also the direction in which you are planning to take your business and your ultimate goals and aims. Try to find an accountant on recommendation, ideally from someone who's business position is similar to your own, and make sure you think of yourself as working with rather than against your accountant. Do as much of the paperwork yourself as possible. Not only will this cost you less, it will also enable you to see exactly where you are spending your money and help you discipline yourself in areas where you are prone to overspend.

Paying the right price

The key to a successful development is to pay the right money for the right property and then to do the right work to it. Sounds simple! Working out what the 'right money' is becomes easier as you get to know how much any given property is likely to be worth when finished and how much it will cost to do the work.

Most professional developers work to a 20% profit margin. This means that when every single item spent on developing the property is deducted they are left with a 20% gross profit on the total investment. Remember property development is a business, and so for every decision you make, you should keep this 20% profit figure firmly at the front of your mind. With any property, you calculate your profit by subtracting all the renovation and purchase costs (including all administrative costs) from your potential selling price. When you find a property that on paper looks like it could be a great deal,, make sure you work systematically through the following calculation:

- **Check potential resale price** of the property (see below, 'What is the ceiling price for your property?')
- **Work out realistic costs for of all works** including all your professional costs
- **Subtract renovation and purchase costs** from potential selling price to give profit

Potential resale value	£120,000
Total cost of works and fees	£30,000
Maximum price you can afford to pay	£70,000
Gross profit of 20% of 100,000	£20,000

The maximum resale value (ceiling price) is £120,000. To achieve your gross profit of 20% you must therefore spend no more than £100,000. You have calculated out that the cost of works will be £30,000, therefore the maximum price you should pay for the unmodernised property is £70,000.

 ## What is the ceiling price for your property?

The ceiling price is the highest price achieved for a similar property in the same area. The best way to establish the ceiling price for your property, therefore, is to find out what similar properties have actually sold for in that area. Beware of simply looking in agents' windows and taking the price at face value – this may be the price the agent *hopes* to achieve but is not the price at which it actually sells. Make sure you are totally realistic about your property when comparing it to others. Is it similar in *every* way, or is it a similar layout but in a different street with different surroundings?

To break through this ceiling price you'll have to do something pretty spectacular with your property... And you'll need a bit of luck too. Be careful not to confuse a rising market with breaking the ceiling price (see box, 'Buying in a rising market', page 25).

Working out your budget

Cost analysis is essential to any business and is a key element of property development. The irony is that your property will be worth considerably less than you paid for it as soon as you start working on it and ripping it apart, though the potential added value of such work can be enormous.

Setting a realistic budget

I cannot stress enough how important it is to set a realistic budget and stick to it. As you will see from the case studies in this book, few of our novice property developers abided by this rule, and they ended up going over budget, often dramatically. There is nothing worse than running out of money and being unable to finish the project. A realistic costing means you are protecting your profit. Otherwise you will end up doing the project for fun rather than for money. Property development is first and foremost a business. It may well be fun at times, but fun alone is not going to pay the bills.

You have already worked out how much you can afford to spend to ensure you end up with your 20% profit. Obviously it doesn't matter at all if you spend less than this figure, it's just essential that you don't spend more. Your next step is to estimate accurately all your building costs. There are a number of guidebooks used by professionals in the building industry that give guides as to building costs, and they are updated regularly. Among them are *Spon's Architects' and Builders' Pricebook* (published by E & FN Spon) and the *Wessex Guides* (published by Wessex Electronic Publishing). They also give estimated current costs per square metre for newbuild. Working out how much it costs to refurbish an *existing* dwelling is more tricky, as it depends on the specific work needed. As a general guide, however, an existing dwelling needing a new roof, wiring, plumbing and complete redecoration is likely to cost about 75% per square metre of the price of newbuild.

Next, sit down and write a detailed list of all your intended work, and then add in ALL the extras, as shown in the Cost Analysis on page 45. The profit figure you come up with is not a real profit if you don't include your stamp duty, estate agent's fees and borrowing costs, even if this does make you feel richer on paper! The main way people run over budget is by not setting a realistic one in the first place, and this is often because they forget to add in (or choose to overlook) these various administrative expenses.

The starting point for your Cost Analysis should be your Specification (see page 64). Write down each element of your Spec and fill in the figures for each item. Then factor in the items you are supplying yourself and list those administrative 'extras' such as solicitor's fees and stamp duty. Finally, add your all-important contingency of 10% (and, to be entirely accurate, you should add the cost of your time, vehicle use, telephone bills, Internet bills, etc.).

No expense required on the property can afford to be seen simply as an 'extra' – small items can add up to a large percentage of the cost of developing a property and if ignored will lull you into a false sense of profitability on the project. It's gutting to suddenly realise that after all that hard work you actually made no more REAL profit on modernising the property than you would have done sitting on the beach in Spain!

Sticking to your budget

Of course setting your budget is just the first step. Sticking to it is the clincher. Once you have worked out your budget, the figures in front of you are set in stone – keeping to them means protecting your profit. If something does end up costing more than you expected, you can take it out of your contingency section. However, if you're a long way out or a number of different things don't go according to plan, then you will simply have to claw back the money elsewhere (probably by giving up on any free time and doing more yourself). If your budget is beginning to buckle under the strain, here are some tips to get it back under control.

- Sanding floors is not necessarily cheaper than carpeting, as the main cost of sanding is the sandpaper, varnish and time. Carpets are making a comeback. This is partly for their warmth and comfort but also because research has shown that an increase in the cases of asthma in children may be caused by lack of exposure to the waste from the dust mites that are in abundance in the carpets that small children crawl around on.

- Tiles can be cheaper than laminate floors.

- You can line rough walls with thick 1000-grade lining paper to avoid having to replaster them, but be aware that this will never give you the perfect finish. Instead you'll have to make the rest of the design scheme work around this more rustic look.

- Don't pull up any plants in your garden until you are absolutely convinced they have to go. Think about replanting them if you feel they are in the wrong place – established plants are very expensive.

- Reuse the existing pan of a loo and only replace the cistern (if necessary), the flush handle and the seat – the pan is the most expensive part to replumb.

- Use thicker worktops in the kitchen – 40-mm worktops look more expensive than the extra cost they involve and make the kitchen look like it has a top-quality finish.

Get ahead	Your contingency is the amount of money you have to fall back on should something come up unexpectedly during the running of the project – you CANNOT afford to omit this from your budget. Think of it as an essential cost rather than an unnecessary luxury.

Cost Analysis

JOB QUOTE

1. Repointing	£500
2. Fitting windows and sills	£700
3. Drainage	£150
4. Fencing	£200
5. Garden landscaping	£600
6. Flat roofs	£350
7. Slate roofs	£1,200
8. Flashing	£50
9. Guttering	£185
10. Timber treatment for woodworm infestation	£430
11. Rising damp remedial works	£1,115
12. Internal walls – add or remove?	£300
13. Chimneybreast – add or remove?	£250
14. Flooring – concrete and/or wood?	£600
15. Electrics – sockets/ switches (including dimmers) /telephone points/intercom /alarm	£1,400
16. Plumbing – radiators/boiler /bathroom/kitchen	£5,300
17. Plastering	£600
18. Joinery – skirtings/cupboards /doors/boxing	£1,500
19. Decorations – inside and outside	£3,530
20. Skips and waste	£950

NOT SUPPLIED BY CONTRACTOR

Carpets	£2,500
Kitchen units and worktops	£1,700
Kitchen appliances	£480
Bathroom suite (including taps!)	£520
Kitchen and bathroom splashbacks	£85

ADMINISTRATIVE

Fees to solicitor for the purchase and sale of the property	£800
Stamp duty on the purchase (if property costs £60,000 or more)	£2,500
Estate agent's fees for the sale	£6,700
Borrowing fees	£7,550
Other administrative costs	£1,200

Contingency 10%
£4,396.50

TOTAL
£4,8361.60

Paying the right price for a property

Jonathan Topps, 42 years old, got into property development because he had very little money following his divorce a few years earlier. His aim was to get back onto the property ladder and secure the house of his dreams without having to depend on anyone else.

Jonathan bought a tired Victorian terrace and gave it a dose of much-needed tender loving care.

The Budget £

Property bought for	£127,500
Projected cost of works	£20,000
Projected sale price	£170,000
Projected gross profit	£22,500 (15.3%)

What he bought

Jonathan bought a typical terraced property that certainly needed modernising, but was it suitable as a profitable development? The house had two reception rooms in the main body of the house, a small reception room towards the rear, which you needed to walk through to get to the kitchen, and beyond this the house's only bathroom, also accessed through the kitchen. Upstairs there were three bedrooms, two of which were big enough to be considered double rooms.

Although Sydenham is only 15 minutes from the city, it has still not reached the dizzy heights of fashionability of somewhere like Notting Hill. Consequently, house prices are still relatively low and there are bargains to be had. Because of the low prices, the child-friendly park and the good schools, young families are attracted to the area and it is this market that Jonathan needed to target with his house. Young families would also be attracted to the type of property that Jonathan had bought – a house with a garden for the young children to play in and enough rooms for them to amuse themselves, scatter their toys and make a mess, plus private rooms, where the grown-ups could relax, and a large bathroom.

The plan

Jonathan recognised that developing property meant thinking about how modern-day buyers want to live and that by moving the bathroom upstairs into the smallest bedroom he would automatically make the property more attractive to his particular market. He also decided to make the third reception room, the kitchen and the existing downstairs bathroom into one lovely big kitchen that overlooked the garden. In this way he made the kitchen one of the house's main selling points.

Jonathan staged his garden attractively by placing a table and chairs in one corner and including an inviting hammock.

By demolishing the lean-to bathroom, Jonathan improved the outlook of his kitchen considerably. Now it could overlook the newly landscaped garden.

Creating a 'catch-all' budget

Developers can make money from any property, in any location and in any condition, but only if they purchase the property for the right price. Never buy a property without working out how much you can sell it for once you have done all the renovations (the ceiling price). If you have invested in an old property similar to Jonathan's, it is essential you account for costs that could crop up – the roof, the drains, the plastering – through comprehensive research and a heavy dose of realism with regard to your budget. If Jonathan had done his sums early on, he would have realised that once he had subtracted his purchasing and renovation costs, and included stamp duty, solicitor's fees and other expenses, he would have been looking at least another £6,000 on top of his original costing.

My advice

I agreed with Jonathan that he needed to target his property at young families and move the bathroom upstairs (neither you, or your young child are going to appreciate the stairs in the middle of the night), and that he needed to open up the back of the house to provide an open-plan kitchen/dining space and garden. I also advised him to:

DO THE JOB PROPERLY. Jonathan needed to deal with all major problems, including the roof, before thinking about fixtures and fittings.

GIVE THE BUYER OPTIONS. It would have been best to have left the living areas as two separate rooms, and to fit doors between the two. This would have given his buyers the flexibility of having two separate or one larger living room.

KEEP IT SIMPLE. Jonathan needed to make the kitchen, bathroom and general decoration classic and simple – young families would appreciate a focus on the practical and would neither desire nor require anything too fancy.

Jonathan's profit was already in trouble from the minute he signed his exchange papers. He had paid too much for his property considering the cost of the work that needed to be done and the ceiling price for similar properties in the area. This was a property that needed major work, and Jonathan made the mistake of not getting a survey done when he bought it. The surveyor would have told him that the house needed a new roof, which would have set him back at least another £6,000.

Jonathan also budgeted much less than he was finally quoted for works (drains, windows and general decorating), which increased his budget by another £15,000. In fact, Jonathan only factored in all the costs of the development once the project was well and truly underway. As he'd failed to research the market thoroughly enough, he was never going to make a huge profit. Nevertheless, he could have salvaged the situation to some extent by spending money only on what was absolutely necessary.

By knocking through the back of the house and moving the bathroom upstairs, Jonathan created enough space for a kitchen/breakfast room. He also united the kitchen and garden by adding French doors.

Instead, he insisted on installing a separate walk-in shower in the bathroom. In this Jonathan made the mistake of bringing his personal taste into the project. He had paid for what he wanted and not what his buyer needed or demanded. He also decided to have expensive appliances in the kitchen and a dishwasher and washing machine all built in. In the living room he fitted an unnecessarily expensive, elaborate fireplace and a skylight in the kitchen extension. Within his extremely tight budget he only had one option – to stick to what was required for the property and forget all those little luxuries.

Halfway through the project, Jonathan was sadly made redundant. Although he was worried about the situation in which he found himself, there was no real panic as he had a very low mortgage and had wisely set aside a contingency to support himself. He decided to use his time as efficiently as possible and spend most days at the

Ideally, all properties should have an upstairs bathroom. Jonathan was absolutely correct for his market to lose his third small bedroom and replace it with a modern contemporary bathroom.

house, but also to attend a course about starting your own business that he hoped would help him on his way to becoming a successful professional property developer. This was a great use of his unexpected free time and showed that he was serious about what he was doing.

Final sums

Property bought for	£127,500
Final cost of works:	
Kitchen and bathroom	£6,400
Roof	£6,500
Modernisation	£6,804
Contractors	£11,116
Decoration	£4,500
Professional fees	£6,479
Total	**£41,799**
Target selling price	£190,000
Target gross profit	**£20,701 (12.2%)**

Jonathan did a fantastic job of renovating his property. The finished house looked amazing and any buyer would thoroughly enjoy the product that Jonathan had created. However, as a money-making exercise, the project didn't go particularly well because in the end Jonathan spent more than double his initial budget, which needed to be kept at the original level to enable him to make a worthwhile profit on the work he had done. **(2002)**

Where are they now?

Jonathan decided to stay in the house for three months after finishing the work in the hope that the market would continue to rise. **(2002)**

3
ESSENTIAL BUILDING WORKS

Once you have worked out a strict budget for your development and the cost of the renovations you will need to do, it's time to think in more detail about how you will actually go about those works and who you'll need to call on to help you. This chapter looks at essential building works, such as major improvements and damp treatment, explains the importance and nature of the various different surveys on offer and gives you a crash course in site project management and how to create happy working relationships with contractors.

Assessing what needs to be done

You will already have given some thought to the amount and type of work needed in the course of working out your budget. In fact, the work you'll need to do on a property will affect your choice of property in the first place. The most important thing is to be realistic about the work you can take on yourself.

How much do you know?

When assessing the work needed on your property you should be guided by two things. First is your current building knowledge. Think carefully about every aspect of what you are about to take on. Are you confident that you can cope with re-roofing a five-bedroomed house or would you be better off cutting your teeth with property development on a flat that needs only interior refurbishment? Remember, you need some knowledge yourself in order to be able to check the work of others.

Second is the type of market you are familiar with. Do you understand what is expected in terms of the style of building and refurbishment by your target market?

I have been exposed to building sites and the process of building all my life and this experience has taught me that you can never know enough. When we started developing we took on a two-bedroomed flat that needed not a great deal more than general redecoration, as this corresponded to the extent of our knowledge at the time.

As you become more accustomed to developing property you will learn a lot from watching builders and other contractors – as well as a certain amount from your own trial and error. If you gradually learn about each separate element of your trade it is easier to understand the whole process and to judge the quality of the work of those you hire. Not to mention that if you start small and hate the whole concept of developing it's a lot quicker and easier to get out of it.

As I've explained, the amount and type of work you choose to do will depend on your existing knowledge. However, there are some issues that must never be overlooked. These are major works and, unless you are a trained surveyor, I would advise you against trying to assess what is needed on your own. You can find out a certain amount simply by looking at the building; beyond that you'll need to call in the experts. Major works are generally split into the following categories:

Subsidence and movement

Stand back as far as you can from the front and back of the property. Check to see if the windows and ridge are level, the walls vertical and if there are any obvious cracks in the brickwork. Then go inside the property and see if you can spot any major cracks in the plasterwork.

Many Victorian buildings were mass-produced with little regard for the type of subsoil and consequently the foundations were not necessarily adequate. This means that inevitably they have a tendency to move around a bit. If the subsoil is clay, then in a very dry summer or a very wet winter, the ground will expand and contract and cracks in the walls will appear. Generally the solution is to dig out underneath the walls and foundations of the building and pour in concrete, which effectively adds more substantial foundations to the existing walls of the property and so makes them less vulnerable to the effects of changing moisture levels in the ground. This process is known as underpinning. It may also be necessary to 'tie' the building together in order to ensure it retains its structural integrity. (An example of a tie is the metal crosses you sometimes see on the flank wall of a building, which acts as a brace.)

Don't immediately panic if there is evidence of previous movement in your property as most buildings will have at least some. The important thing is that the property is not still moving. The good news is that if a building has stayed up for 100 years or so it is unlikely to be going anywhere fast (unless there is a mine or river running underneath it!).

If the property has not been decorated for years this actually works to your advantage when checking for evidence of movement, as it's much easier to see exactly what has been going on with the building. Redecoration can mask many problems. If you suspect your property has structural problems you will need to instruct a structural surveyor to find out precisely what is going on. The survey will tell you whether the movement is historic or current and the surveyor will recommend the best way to stabilise it. Some types of movement in a building can affect its insurance status and unless the issue is completely resolved before you put the property on the market it will inevitably have a negative impact on your sale time and price, as buyers or their mortgage companies, often unnecessarily in my opinion, feel it is safer to steer clear.

Damp and timber problems

Does any area of the building smell strange? Can you spot any damp patches on the walls or ceilings? Are there salts (resembling a thin layer of cotton wool) coming out of the brickwork or plasterwork? Do any of the floors feel spongy when you walk on them? Is there any mushroom-like fungus around?

If you spot any of the above signs I would always advise that you get a specialist damp and timber survey carried out by a reputable company that has been recommended to you by a good local estate agent. Even if your property does not betray any of the tell-tale signs of damp, a survey is still a sensible precaution. The service is sometimes free of charge. The damp and timber company will confirm whether your fears are justified, whether any work needs to be done on the property, and will issue you with a guarantee once the work has been carried out. It is essential that you keep this guarantee in a safe place – that way when you come to sell your property you can pass it on to your purchasers as proof that any damp- and timber-related issues that did come up were properly dealt with. Damp and timber guarantees are typically for 25 years.

⮕ The roof

Stand back from the roof and compare it to other roofs. Are there any slipped slates? Does the flashing (bit down the sides) look worn and old? Is there grass or plants growing out of it? Go out when it is pouring with rain. Do the gutters carry the water down the drainpipe or is water falling out of any of the joints? If the answer to any of these questions is yes then you need to call in a roofer to sort out the problem. You should expect to pay between £3,000 and £6,000 for a new roof with two lead valleys. Tiles are at the cheaper end and slate at the more expensive end. If you are replacing slate with tiles you may have to strengthen the roof timbers. It's also worth bearing in mind that you are losing another original feature.

> ## Beat the competition
>
> There is no point in glossing over any damp or timber problems; they'll come back to haunt you. Deal with them while the property is still a building site to keep costs down, and ask the company doing the work to tell you ways of bringing down the cost of the treatment (e.g. taking up the floorboards for them before they spray for woodworm and hacking off the plaster ready for them to replaster).

⮕ The plumbing

The general rule is that if the plumbing works then it's probably OK. You need to have radiators in every room and a modern boiler (see pages 109 to 110). Make sure everything is properly insulated and have your boiler serviced. If you are having problems with water pressure, are not getting hot water, the pilot light keeps going out, or radiators or pipes are leaking then you may need to call in a plumber. Expect to pay between £3,000 and £5,000 to replumb a property with one bathroom and one kitchen (including the installation of central heating). If the mains feed between the road and your property is lead and you decide to replace it, this can cost an extra £300 or so, though most water companies will give you a free lead pipe replacement if you are removing the leadwork within your property.

⮕ The wiring

Try to find out from the seller when the property was last rewired and, if in doubt, instruct a qualified electrician to check the wiring is up to standard. Rewiring a three-bed house usually costs between £2,500 and £3,000.

➲ The windows

If your windows are rotten or substandard you may have to replace either one or both sashes (the parts that slide up and down) or the whole box (the wooden part that the sashes sit in). Windows, as I am sure you will have noticed, come in all different shapes and sizes. But one thing is for sure – the wrong windows in the wrong property and the wrong area will undoubtedly damage the value of your property dramatically. Take time to research the area thoroughly and see what type of windows the majority of the more expensive houses in the area have. Or ask your estate agent which types are more popular. UPVC double-glazed windows command a premium for some properties while in others they can actually devalue the property so much that it pays to take them back out and refit original windows. In properties built after about 1920 it is often considered that replacing original windows with UPVC double-glazed windows may improve them. It is also almost always considered best to replace steel windows (often made by a company called Crittall). This is largely because steel windows tend to be badly insulated and are also prone to condensation, with the accompanying tendency to rust. Recent legislation for thermal regulation of replacement windows states that if you are replacing any of the window apart from the actual glass you must have double-glazing fitted – the window does not have to change greatly in appearance but must be altered to house this thicker glass unit.

The survey

Surveys can be more or less comprehensive, depending on how much information you require and how much you want to spend – ask your surveyor exactly what you'll be getting for your money and make sure you commission your surveyor BEFORE you find your property. This will avoid any unnecessary delays.

A survey will be required and commissioned automatically by your mortgage company. However, this is really just a simple valuation (often called the Basic Valuation), the purpose of which is to check the bank's equity is safe in the property (i.e. the property is worth at least as much as the bank has agreed to lend you). Most lenders will have a panel of local surveyors from whom they will be happy to accept a Basic Valuation, but if you feel that your property needs a more far-reaching survey, then you will need to organise it yourself. These more comprehensive surveys are of two types, the 'Flat or Homebuyer's' survey or the 'Full Structural' survey. Again, your mortgage broker or estate agent will be able to recommend a reputable company they have worked with before.

YORKSHIRE
Building Society
MEMBERSHIP HAS BENEFITS

VALUATION REPORT FOR MORTGAGE
PREPARED for YORKSHIRE BUILDING SOCIETY
APPLICANT'S COPY

Valuers Ref: Branch: Account No:

1. Name(s) of Applicant(s)	

2. Address of Property
(Including Postcode)

168 GIPSY ROAD

This valuation report has been prepared to enable the Society to assess whether there is sufficient security for the loan required. It is **NOT** to advise you upon whether you should purchase or to provide a schedule of repairs. If you require this information you **MUST** arrange your own survey.

3. Description
a) Type of Property

House	Bungalow	Chalet	Detached	Semi Detached	Terrace	Flat or Maisonette	On Which Floor	No. of Floors in Block
						F	GRD	2

PTYPE

b) Property Use (If other than a single private dwelling)

PUSE

c) Construction (More than one box will apply)

If non-traditional full details should be provided in General Observations Sec. 9

SC

	Walls				Roof					
Brick (1)	Stone (2)	Timber Framed (3)	Other (4)	Slate (5)	Stone (6)	Tile (7)	Other (8)	Apex (9)	Flat and Felt Roof Less than 50% (10)	More than 50% (11)
X				X						

d) Accommodation
Please state number of

Rec. Rooms	Kitchens	Bedrooms	Bathrooms	Inside W.C.s	Basement Rooms	Attic Rooms	Out-buildings	Garages	If no garage is there garage space ?
1	1	1	1	1					No

e) If there is a garage, state type and construction

Services

Drainage	Electricity	Gas	Water	Central Heating please specify type
MAINS	MAINS	MAINS	MAINS	GAS

f) Total Superficial Area (all floors of main building measured externally)

53 sq metres

g) Date Property Built

1900 circ   Stage reached if being built   State if NHBC Registered

h) If recently built, or in the course of construction, state name of builder

4. Tenure
a) Freehold, Leasehold or Feudal
b) Ground rent, Chief rent or Feu Duty
c) Details of any Escalating Ground Rent

Leasehold   If Leasehold, state years unexpired   85
£ Not known   p.a.

5. Roads
a) Are all roadways and pavements abutting the property completed to the Local Authority's satisfaction?

YES   X   NO

b) If NO, what works are required, who is liable for, and what is the estimated cost of, completion?

6. Property Insurance Recommended

Note: Main Building includes walls, gates, hedges, fences, paths, drives, terraces, and swimming pools

Cost of rebuilding inc. demolition, site clearance, professional fees and Local Authority requirements.

Main Building	Garage	Outbuilding
£ 46,000	£	£

7. Valuation
a) Basis of Valuation

Vacant Possession   X   Part Possession   Investment

b) Do you recommend the property as suitable security for a mortgage advance from the Society?

YES   X   NO

If NO, please state your reasons in Section 9.

If YES, what is its value for mortgage purposes

GROSS VALUE   £ 60,000

Less Reserve for Outstanding Streetworks (See Section 5b)   £
Less Reserve for Essential Repairs (See Section 9)   £
NET VALUE FOR MORTGAGE PURPOSES   £ 60,000

c) Present Value, including site if being built

£

8. Date of Valuation

9th April, 1999 - C V O - STAFF

YBS 18

Please complete section 9 attached, 'General Observations' and the Declaration.
Return the Report to the Society along with the copies for the District Office, Applicant and Conveyancer.

6/98

9. General Observations
Valuers are invited to make fullest use of this section. Comments should include a description of the neighbourhood together with any factors which may affect the future value of the property. Defects should be enumerated and it should be clearly stated whether attention to such defects should be a condition of the mortgage advance or undertaken before any advance is made.

This valuation report has been prepared by a Staff Valuation Surveyor employed by Yorkshire Building Society

At the time of inspection the property was carpeted and furnished and this prevented an inspection of certain areas of the fabric of the building. The following points were noted:-
1. The property has suffered from previous structural movement in the form of distortion to the flank elevations. For mortgage purposes, it is felt that the matter will be acceptable but nevertheless, the possibility of further movement occurring in the future cannot be completely discounted. 2. Cracking is apparent to the pathways around the rear drainage chamber and the applicant may consider it prudent to have the drains tested by a competent plumber. 3. The slate roof covering is showing signs of general wear/deterioration. 4. In view of the age of the property the applicant may consider it prudent to have the flat inspected by a reputable timber and damp specialist and have any recommendations executed under a long term meaningful guarantee. 5. Solicitors should be asked to confirm that adequate covenants are contained, within the lease, regarding such matters as repair, maintenance, rights of support, insurance etc. Solicitors also to confirm that an unexpired lease term of at least 75 years exists.

From a superficial inspection the property generally appears maintained to a satisfactory standard commensurate with its age and in good decorative repair. There would appear to be no repair items outstanding of an essential nature for mortgage purposes.

The property is considered to represent suitable security for mortgage purposes at the valuation given overleaf.

GO1
GO2
GO3
GO4
GO5
GO6
GO7
GO8

TO THE APPLICANT(S)
1. The valuation report is not a structural survey or Home Buyer's Report. The valuer has carried out a limited visual inspection only and will not be able to comment upon areas of the property which were covered, unexposed or inaccessible. The services will **NOT** be tested. Only those defects which could significantly affect the Society's security will be referred to.
2. The valuation shown in the report is the figure considered by the valuer to be appropriate for mortgage purposes. This figure may differ from market value. In the case of house purchase no warranty is given, or may be implied, that the purchase price is reasonable.
3. This valuation may have been prepared by a Staff Valuation Surveyor employed by the Society **OR** by an external independent Panel Valuer. If prepared by a Staff Valuation Surveyor a comment to this effect will be included in Section 9 - General Observations.
4. The valuation report is for the use of the Society and information of the applicant(s) only. The contents should not be disclosed to anyone other than the applicant's own professional advisors. The Yorkshire Building Society, together with the valuer (whether an employee of the Society or an external Panel Valuer) accept no responsibility for any loss suffered by applicants due to reliance upon this report, or the valuation.
IMPORTANT
IT IS YOUR OWN RESPONSIBILITY TO ENSURE YOU ARE FULLY AWARE OF THE CONDITION OF THE PROPERTY YOU ARE BUYING BEFORE LEGAL COMMITMENT. IT IS ALWAYS RECOMMENDED THAT YOU ARRANGE YOUR OWN INDEPENDENT SURVEY. IF YOU FAIL TO DO SO YOU SHOULD BE AWARE OF THE RISKS YOU ARE TAKING.

This survey is an example of a Flat or Homebuyer's survey for a leasehold property. It goes into some detail about structural movement, cracking, roof deterioration, etc., but the emphasis is on 'suggesting' areas of possible problems and recommending consultations with specialists, rather than pinpointing precise problems and offering specific solutions. For this more in-depth information you would need to opt for a Full Structural survey (see box, over).

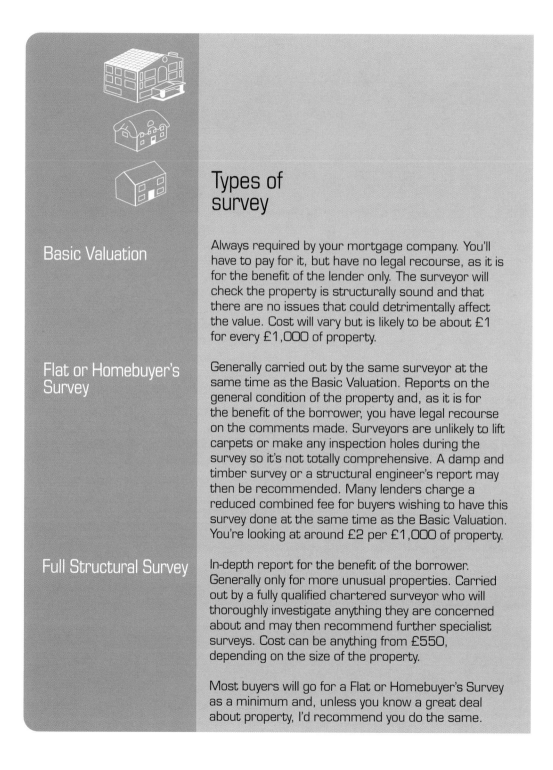

Types of survey

Basic Valuation

Always required by your mortgage company. You'll have to pay for it, but have no legal recourse, as it is for the benefit of the lender only. The surveyor will check the property is structurally sound and that there are no issues that could detrimentally affect the value. Cost will vary but is likely to be about £1 for every £1,000 of property.

Flat or Homebuyer's Survey

Generally carried out by the same surveyor at the same time as the Basic Valuation. Reports on the general condition of the property and, as it is for the benefit of the borrower, you have legal recourse on the comments made. Surveyors are unlikely to lift carpets or make any inspection holes during the survey so it's not totally comprehensive. A damp and timber survey or a structural engineer's report may then be recommended. Many lenders charge a reduced combined fee for buyers wishing to have this survey done at the same time as the Basic Valuation. You're looking at around £2 per £1,000 of property.

Full Structural Survey

In-depth report for the benefit of the borrower. Generally only for more unusual properties. Carried out by a fully qualified chartered surveyor who will thoroughly investigate anything they are concerned about and may then recommend further specialist surveys. Cost can be anything from £550, depending on the size of the property.

Most buyers will go for a Flat or Homebuyer's Survey as a minimum and, unless you know a great deal about property, I'd recommend you do the same.

Labour relations

Good working relationships with everyone who works on your property will speed up your project and get you nearer your profit faster. Depending on the type of property and the work you want done, you may not need to employ the whole range of different contractors but one thing you will need to decide is whether to project manage the work yourself or to delegate this to someone else.

The project manager

The role of project manager is one of the most important on a building site. The project manager runs the whole job, from start to finish and has overall responsibility for anyone working on the site. He or she must ensure that the site complies with any permissions and building regulations (see pages 90 to 93), order all materials and supplies and make sure these are not on site too early (cluttering up the site and getting damaged) and not too late. In addition, the project manager must check that each individual tradesman is booked in and that all contractors turn up in the right order, at the right time, and that all work remains within the budget and timescale agreed. On the financial side, the project manager is responsible for paying the subcontractors' wages and dealing with their tax.

As you can imagine, this is an extremely time-consuming job. It involves being on site for several hours a day, making numerous phone calls every day, and will almost always be a six-, if not seven-, day week job, with a 7.00 a.m. start.

The project manager is at both the top and the bottom of the pecking order on a building site – the one making decisions and employing the subcontractors, but also the one running around after everyone else, clearing up the site and making sure everyone is provided with tea, coffee and lavatory facilities. Moreover, it is invariably the project manager who will be the one putting in the extra hours when the site is running behind.

Doing your own project management

When you consider the workload of the project manager, it should come as no surprise that the cost of such a person is often 10% of the cost of the whole project. So, do you pay someone to carry out this role for you or do you attempt to make a saving by tackling it yourself?

If you honestly feel that you are up to the challenge of project management then go for it. Some of the novice developers featured in the series have successfully project managed their own site with little or no prior experience. But remember, you will only be saving money if you complete the project satisfactorily. Changing tack halfway through a project will probably cost you as much as you might have saved, but with a whole lot more hassle. If you have a very busy full-time job then project managing yourself is not a realistic option. If your arrangements are more flexible then it might be realistic, but you must think long and hard about how much time you will need to sacrifice. If your time on site is preventing you from having a successful career elsewhere then the choice is harder to make.

If you do decide to go ahead here are some tips:

• Source all the materials you need as soon as you exchange on your purchase – the period between exchange and completion is a perfect time to get the site organised and ready to go.

• Keep a wallchart showing exactly when each subcontractor is working and how subcontractors overlap with each other. The key to running subcontractors well is timing. If your plasterer has booked you in for a 5-day slot on Tuesday it is not much good if your electrician has not finished his first fix wiring by Monday night!

• Have back-up telephone numbers for an alternative electrician, plumber, plasterer, carpenter and decorator.

• Develop good working relationships. It is essential you establish a good rapport with your subcontractors. Be attentive to their needs and be firm but fair if things seem to be going off course.

• Keep calm. If things go wrong, take a deep breath and try to think logically towards a workable solution.

The best piece of advice I can give is to be realistic about your time. If you know deep down you can't project manage this time, there's always the next. We've all had that experience of going to see a friend who is in the middle of a major 'home improvement' project, desperate to keep you out of the living room where lurks an embarrassing DIY failure that has cost him or her a lot of time and money and has almost certainly devalued the home. If you know you can't do something, don't try. Get someone else to do it and get on with a job you ARE good at.

Finding a builder

A terrible myth has evolved in this country that all builders are baddies – while I cannot pretend that all builders are goodies, it is also fair to say that often it is the *employer* that is the real cause of building nightmares, usually because of lack of knowledge, inexperience and sheer bloody-mindedness!

One thing you can be sure about is that if you choose the wrong builder you will go quietly and slowly round the bend. Not only will your sanity be at risk, so too will the thousands of pounds of capital you have so carefully invested into the project. If you are employing someone to project manage your site (the main contractor) then in some ways you have less of a problem because you only need to find *one* person who is right. However, in some ways you have more of a problem because if you choose the wrong main contractor then all the other contractors may well by extension be wrong.

So where do you find the right builder? Personal recommendation is always your best bet. If a friend or neighbour can recommend a contractor they have recently used then there's a good chance things will go smoothly. Failing this, ask your estate agent if they can recommend anyone or see if any nearby properties are having similar work done and boldly enquire. One particularly useful website is www.improveline.com, which offers an easy way to find a suitable, recommended builder anywhere in the UK. Looking in *Yellow Pages* or in trade magazines is risky. These are ads – of course it sounds marvellous! A better guide, although not a guarantee, is to see whether a builder belongs to a body that encourages its members to adopt good standards of work. Among these are the Federation of Master Builders (FMB) and the Guild of Master Craftsmen. Always get quotes from at least three different builders, and don't necessarily go for the cheapest. The following quality-control test will help you choose.

- Ask what other contracts the builder has running and what stage they are at – an overstretched builder who has several other projects on the go at similar stages should set the alarm bells ringing.

- Ask to see the builder's last job and speak to their employer to check all went smoothly – a good track record counts for a lot.

- Check whether you will receive guarantees for re-roofing/re-wiring/re-plumbing /damp work. Contractors should be happy to provide these and they are a bonus when you come to sell and have this paperwork to hand.

The success of your relationship with your builders in some cases is as much down to you as to them. Incomplete or vague instructions will damage the relationship. Work out EXACTLY what you want done before you ask a builder to quote (see 'Writing a specification' on page 64) and NEVER let contractors start work before this is crystal clear to all involved. Indecision will cost the builder and by extension cost you. Always be fair about extras – if you decide the avocado suite you bought was not such a good idea after it has been plumbed in this is your fault. Equally, if goods you are responsible for ordering are not on site on time then there's no reason why you should not pay for your lack of organisation. Lastly, ensure you do not under or overpay your builder for works done to date – either way, you'll end up with no builder at all.

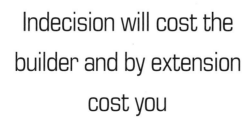

Indecision will cost the builder and by extension cost you

Writing a specification

A clear and detailed specification is essential for the smooth running of any building project. A specification is a written list of precisely what you want done that you give to each builder who quotes. The clearer you are about what you want the more accurate the quote will be and the more tightly you can control your overall budget.

In essence your Spec is similar to your Cost Analysis (see page 45), but with additional information about each job you want done and drawings of what you require where necessary. You can never give too much information in your Spec. Try to put yourself in your contractors' place and assess your requirements from their perspective. If you ask them to 'fit a kitchen' that could involve anything from 5 to 35 units flatpacked or pre-built, and could mean working with awkward gaps or all fitting easily. Naturally, the contractor will quote for the upper end, just in case you actually do decide on a bizarre combination of cork and chrome hand-built units! The one to lose out is you because the vagueness of your Spec has prevented you from getting an accurate quote and you may subsequently go over budget.

At the bottom of the Specification write down all the items that you are supplying yourself. Ask your builder to confirm that this is everything he is expecting you to supply and make him specify the dates on which he requires each item. (Then make sure you order in plenty of time!) Ensure your builder understands that site security and cleanliness are of paramount importance in order to avoid theft and problems with neighbours. As all properties are different every specification will naturally be different too. A good idea is to split your Spec up into a few main headings, corresponding to the different areas of the property, and the different types of work required, and then subheadings within each main heading.

Example:

EXTERNAL WORKS

Demolition of unwanted building mass
Extensions to be built
External doors and windows removed, installed or altered
Repointing or re-rendering (specified by area or meterage)

INTERNAL HARD SIDE WORKS

Demolition of internal walls
Installation of new internal walls
Plastering (specified by area or meterage)
Floors to be concreted or screeded

ROOF WORKS

Roof conversion
Reproofing

Gutter repair or replacement
Valley and flashing repair or replacement
Installation of Velux windows
Chimneystack repair, removal or alteration
Roof timbers repaired or replaced

JOINERY
Staircase repair, replacement or alteration
Doors and doorways altered or replaced
Cupboards built or altered
Boxing around exposed services and fitments
Skirting, architraves, sills and thresholds altered, repaired or renewed

Further headings may include:
DAMP PROOFING AND TIMBER TREATMENT
PLUMBING WORKS
ELECTRICAL WORKS
FLOOR FINISHES
GARDEN LANDSCAPING

Getting on with your neighbours

In my experience the majority of human beings are reluctant to accept change in any form, regardless of whether that change represents an improvement or not. As a property developer you must be sensitive to this and do whatever you can to ensure disturbances and inconvenience for your neighbours during the few months of building work are kept to a minimum. Be up front. Explain to them what you are doing so that they don't have to guess – uncertainty breeds suspicion. Offer to clean their windows if you are doing very dusty work and keep the pavement outside clear and swept.

See Resources (pages 167 to 173) for a list of building suppliers.

You can never give
too much information
in your Spec

Change of use

Renovating agricultural buildings can be a very risky undertaking, but get it right and you really could be quids in.

Make-up artist Philip and trainee barrister Stephen are two men with a great sense of design and style who gave up their jobs and life in London to launch themselves into careers in property development. Both had a very clear idea of what they wanted to achieve in terms of the look and feel of the property they bought.

The Budget £

Property bought for	£55,000
Projected cost of works	£55,000
Projected selling price	£180,000
Projected gross profit	£70,000 (63.6%)

The boys planned to spend £40,000 on the structural work and just £15,000 on fixtures and fittings (to include a kitchen and three ensuite bathrooms!)

What they bought

This was one of the more ambitious projects seen in *Property Ladder*. Philip and Stephen decided on an old dairy barn in Lincolnshire – a complete shell when they bought it – which they hoped to renovate to be the pilot project of their new development and interior design company. Not surprisingly perhaps, this was a project in which design overtook money. It was their first foray into property development and to tackle such a conversion was a brave decision. Converting an agricultural building into a contemporary home is far from simple but if you are willing to take the chance the results can be amazing and the project highly lucrative.

The dairy was situated in a tiny agricultural village just outside Lincoln. There was a Post Office, pub, butcher's shop and primary school. With a population of just 400, and well away from the tourist route, the location made an ideal rural family retreat (rather than a country pile for wealthy socialites looking to entertain). It was crucial that Philip and Stephen marketed the property towards a traditional family and to local people as well as outsiders.

When buying a property for which you want to change the use, getting planning permission is crucial. If you are buying without permission for change of use, assuming this will be granted halfway through the project, you must at least research the local planning department's legislation to give you a good idea of what their final decision might be. But remember, this is no guarantee. You must also find out whether the property is listed. If so, your designs and materials will need listed building approval – the alteration of the shell of the building will almost certainly be problematic. On the plus side, you can sometimes apply for grants to assist you with the build and there are some VAT advantages that you should check out with your accountant.

Philip and Stephen used all their design skills to create a beautiful home finished to an incredibly high standard.

Project managing

Partly to save money and partly to embrace and learn about their new way of life, Philip and Stephen chose to project manage the site themselves. This is a good idea, but a successful site requires time, contacts, a huge amount of effort and considerable skill (see pages 62 to 64). Before you give up your job make sure you do your sums. If your current salary is more than the cost of hiring a project manager then, unless you really want to do it, stick with the day job and let someone else manage the site. Philip and Stephen gave up their London jobs to concentrate on the development and ran into many unforeseen problems. The project was finally completed two months behind schedule and £30,000 over budget. Bearing in mind they were totally new to the world of developing and that they took on SUCH an ambitious project, they did in fact run the site extremely well. Perhaps a more experienced project manager would have realised that their original timescale and budget were amazingly optimistic, but Stephen and Philip's future projects can only benefit from all the lessons they learnt in the course of their first one.

The plan

Philip and Stephen planned to change the feeding area into a large and spacious lounge and the storage room into a kitchen. The cattle barns would be divided into three ensuite bedrooms and a dining room. With an imported designer Swiss kitchen,

Philip and Stephen mixed and matched their materials in the kitchen, combining contemporary with traditional and so creating a really unique feel.

a glass wall in the dining room and the three ensuites, this property was going to be the height of contemporary designer chic. It also meant they were in danger of shooting way over budget. The mix of contemporary fittings in traditional buildings can work very effectively but the risk of narrowing your market can be high, even if you have ensured there is a demand for your product locally.

My advice

The major issue here was developing a very unusual style of property for the area. I was worried that in this small traditional village it would be more difficult to find a buyer willing to pay top-end prices for a property clearly better suited to a cutting-edge, metropolitan market. Philip and Stephen made the crucial mistake of developing with their own tastes and lifestyle too much in mind and decided not to install a fireplace in the spacious living area, simply because they did not like fireplaces themselves. Having gambled their careers and a lot of money on this property, a quick sale was imperative. My advice was therefore as follows:

SCRAP THE THIRD ENSUITE. This was an expensive luxury that would not actually add any value to the property and could even have done the opposite, by making the third bedroom very small. Stephen and Philip were unconvinced so I advised them to build up the internal partition walls to knee-height to get a feel for the size of their new rooms before going ahead. They soon realised that having a third bathroom was not only wasting space but was also an unnecessary expense. Scrapping it helped their budget – even if they *had* already laid the drains!

DO NOT IGNORE THE ORIGINAL STYLE OF THE BUILDING. OK – so go for cool chic but include traditional features too. I showed them some contemporary

Realising that their market would appreciate a separate dining area, the boys placed a dining table in one of their reception rooms to suggest to the buyer how the room could be used.

wood-burning stoves and they decided to follow my advice and install one that created a focal point that really pulled the design of the living room together. Remember, if you cannot actually sell the house at the end of the project then all the painstaking effort and attention to detail has been for nothing.

KEEP THE BUDGET UNDER CONTROL. It's easy to be seduced by catalogues and showrooms. Stephen and Philip fell in love with a kitchen that cost over £20,000! Considering their original budget for the kitchen was £5,000 this was a massive overspend and one that was extremely unlikely to add the equivalent amount to the asking price. Instead, think about adding to more simple units with good-quality, well-designed handles, worktops and splashbacks. Cleverly designed lighting can also make a huge difference to the atmosphere of a room.

Final sums

Property bought for	£55,000
Final cost of works including fees	**£85,000**
Target selling price	£200,000
Target gross profit	**£60,000 (42.9%)**

It's important to keep to one style throughout your property. This gives a feeling of space and unity. Philip and Stephen carried their 'chic modern mixed with traditional' look through into the bathroom.

Three estate agents valued the property as follows:

Agent 1   £165,000

'The house is too high-tech for the market in that area.'

Agent 2   £200,000

'The house has a quality mix of old style and high-tech design.'

Agent 3   £225,000

'This was a very very high-quality house and the valuation reflects that.'

Philip and Stephen did create a simply magnificent home. It was an extremely ambitious project and could have gone horribly wrong. They faced obstacles ranging from local planning authority restrictions to foot-and-mouth, as well as having the stress of running the site themselves. However, their devotion to style and their eye for design and attention to detail resulted in a superb property that made a great portfolio piece for their new design and development company. **(2001)**

I would always advise that you create a focal point in any living room. Here the wood-burning stove serves the purpose.

Where are they now?

Philip and Stephen's first buyer did a disappearing act after his offer was accepted, so the boys ran a private ad in the *FT* one weekend and had a lot of interest from potential buyers in the south. At one point they were receiving four to five viewings a week. They eventually sold the property some months later for £235,000 – £10,000 more than the top valuation. Since then Stephen and Philip have had design commissions from Sheffield to Paris. **(2002)**

4

SPENDING YOUR BUDGET CORRECTLY —
MAJOR WORKS

You've bought the property and you've done the essential building work. Now it's time to concentrate on the changes you need to make to the interior of the property. In other words, you need to create a comfortable home, with a pleasing yet practical layout, that is suitable in every way for the market you are targeting.

A hassle-free home

Buyers will pay a premium for a property where careful thought has been given to the internal layout and where both the minor and the major building works have been completed to a satisfactory standard. It provides them with exactly what they want – think of your profit as their payment to you for creating their new home for them. If any of these areas have been overlooked, however, then what you have created is not in fact a hassle-free home but a product that is fundamentally flawed.

The importance of layout

Both modernised and unmodernised properties can be found at bargain prices if there is something fundamentally wrong with their layout. The difference between a property that works well for its inhabitants and one that doesn't often comes down to how the internal space is organised. If there is a problem with the layout of your property, your prospective buyer won't necessarily be able to put a finger on what is wrong, but will just get a feeling that it doesn't quite work – and buy elsewhere. A property with a layout that works well, on the other hand, will command a premium and it is therefore essential that you design your space so that it not only looks good but also *feels* right.

A historical perspective

Fashions in architecture and interior design change almost as frequently as fashions in clothes. In Roman times, architecture was essentially symmetrical with classical order, proportion and detail. Since then, we have veered both away from and towards these basic concepts of design.

Many of the Victorian terraces that we see in abundance in our towns and cities today were mass built to house workers that were migrating from the countryside at the time of the Industrial Revolution in the mid-1800s. These terraces were laid out

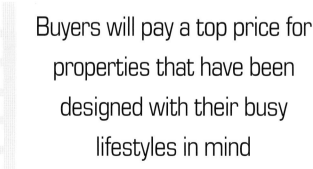

Buyers will pay a top price for properties that have been designed with their busy lifestyles in mind

with ease and cost of build in mind, as well as the limited plumbing expectations of the time. An entire room used only for bathroom activities was not then the norm and loos were considered fairly unhygienic. A small room housing just a loo , therefore, tended to be added onto the back of the main building, behind the kitchen, so enabling an easy run to join the main sewage route that went through the back gardens of the terraces. (This was a far cry from how waste was dealt with up until The Plague and Great Fire of London in 1665 and 1666 respectively, when you would simply chuck the contents of your pot out of an upper-floor window into the street!) The larger Victorian terraces of four or more bedrooms were normally used by the middle classes, who were likely to have a couple of servants either living out or, sometimes, housed on the top floor of the family home, away from the family they served.

Before long people's requirements changed and they began to demand fully plumbed bathrooms. These were generally fitted nearby the existing waste. The Edwardians also realised that it would better suit their lifestyles to have all the rooms of the house to be off one central hallway, and so building designs evolved to suit these new demands.

Today, having a bathroom positioned downstairs behind the kitchen is, understandably, not considered the most logical move (who wants to struggle downstairs in the middle of the night to go to the loo or to smell unpleasant aromas coming from the bathroom when cooking an evening meal!). Many Victorian properties, however, do still have this layout. If yours is such a property, you might want to think about reorganising the space and moving the bathroom upstairs. Our tastes and requirements have evolved considerably and there is now greater emphasis on the design and feel of the interior of properties and on making the space complement the lifestyles we lead. Buyers will pay a top price for properties that have been designed with their busy lifestyles in mind.

Beat the competition

If you are developing a property that has a downstairs bathroom, you will very often attract more buyers if you move it upstairs, even if you lose the smallest bedroom. The bathroom is a 'night-time' room and so should be located close to the other night-time rooms, i.e. the bedrooms.

Designing your space according to your market

How you deal with the space and layout of your property comes down, once again, to your market. Every decision you make on the interior appearance of the property must be made with your market firmly in mind. By observing and thinking about the way in which people live, and providing your market with what it wants, you are more likely to become a successful property developer.

Two into one

A good example of how trends in layout can change is seen with the knocked-through front reception rooms of a Victorian terraced house. Ten years ago, it was practically impossible to sell such a property if these two rooms had not been knocked together. Today, however, you'll find far fewer people frantically knocking down this dividing wall as soon as they get their hands on the property.

One of the reasons for this recent change is that more of us are bringing our work home, therefore requiring separate rooms to suit the living and the working elements of our lives. Lifestyle changes have lead to layout changes.

Similarly, most families with children will agree that they would rather have a playroom-cum-TV room, with the inevitable toys and chocolate-biscuit fingermarks, and a separate grown-up room where things are (one hopes) a wee bit cleaner and tidier, than to have one big messy room.

There's no doubt that knocking through two rooms can give a great sense of space. One good solution to this dilemma, therefore, is to knock through a large doorway and fit double doors on parliament hinges (hinges that enable the door to fold right back to the wall). This means the prospective buyer can decide how they want the layout to work and as such helps you to open up your property to a broader market.

Practical considerations of reorganising space

There are two basic ways to design a new house, from the outside in or from the inside out (with a little bit of overlapping, of course). Three hundred years ago larger houses tended to be designed from the outside in, as an ostentatious exterior that would impress others was considered to be of paramount importance.

Today (and without the cook, housekeeper and maid), ease of living is foremost in people's minds and houses tend therefore to be designed from the inside out. By this I mean that most people will start by saying they want a kitchen this size, a playroom this size, a dining room this size and so on, and an architect will effectively fit the rooms together, rather as if he or she were doing a jigsaw. The last (though crucial) job is to make the front of the property look appealing.

Redesigning *existing* living space is slightly different as there are limitations as to what you can do to the property. The key considerations are the drainage and where it needs to run, and the staircase, which while possible to move, cannot be moved without considerable cost.

Start by drawing each floor to scale on a piece of paper, adding in the staircase and where the existing drainage runs are. Take a copy of this so that the original is safe and start doodling on the copy with layout possibilities. You will be limited by the fact that to make the profit you need you must keep a certain number of bedrooms, bathrooms and living rooms, but you can swap these rooms around, make them bigger/smaller or create or retain corridors to make the space work better for those who will occupy it.

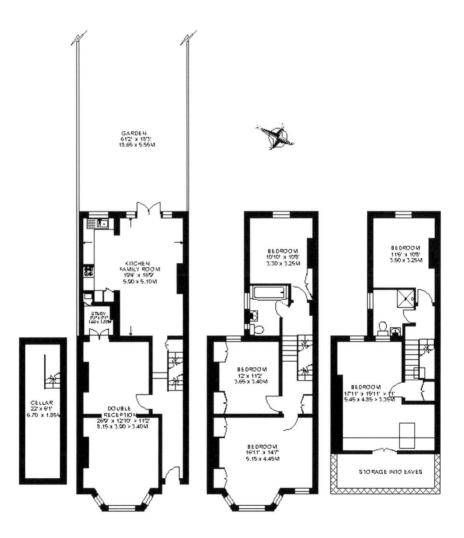

I've stressed that the layout changes you make must be right for your particular market. However, some of these changes will help you attract the highest possible price, whatever the nature of your market.

ROOM ORDER

The rooms in your property can be categorised as either daytime (kitchens and living rooms) or night-time (bathrooms and bedrooms). Always aim to keep daytime rooms and night-time rooms, as far as possible, in separate areas of the property – having the two types muddled up will give the property an awkward feel. If bedrooms and living rooms are next to each other it can be unpleasant for the person who wants to retire to bed when everyone else is still up partying in the living room. The bedroom should be as private a space as possible – if you can, therefore, locate your bedrooms at the back of the property.

ACCESS

Try to avoid a layout which forces you to go through one room to get to another (unless it is an ensuite bathroom for the sole use of the bedroom it adjoins) – it usually doesn't feel right and relegates the room you walk through to little more than a corridor. If this really is unavoidable, perhaps because there is simply not enough width to the property to fit a corridor without losing a room altogether, try to make sure that you are not walking through a daytime room to get to a night-time room, and vice versa.

SIGHT LINES

A sight line means the range of views your eye can take in when you are standing at one particular point and must always be borne in mind with any reorganisation of your space. A disregard for sight lines means your property may not fulfil its potential. For instance, to see as much of the garden as possible from far back into the property you must have large glazed doors at the end of the room that overlooks the garden (very often the kitchen). If you have a side door and can't even see the garden you are unlikely to achieve a similar premium.

WASTED SPACE (OR NOT...)

Do not make the mistake of assuming that landings, hallways or nooks and crannies automatically constitute a waste of space and rush around trying to fill them with cupboards, small items of furniture or other objects. Sometimes leaving spaces empty actually makes a property feel bigger, as it gives the impression that the property has sufficient space to be able to afford to waste some of it! Small empty areas such as these give the property some room to breathe. To decide whether or not you should utilise a specific space consider what else you are offering the buyer and whether you can afford the luxury of not using the space.

Balancing the property: extending and converting

The decision whether to extend your property, either upwards with a loft conversion, downwards into a cellar or outwards with an extension, needs to be considered very carefully. There is a basic premise that by adding square meterage to a property you add value, as property prices are often roughly gauged on price per square metre. In reality, this is only really true when the extension balances the property correctly – if an extension makes the property top- or bottom-heavy its potential added value will be reduced.

Beat the competition

In older properties doors are generally hung so that as you open them you cannot see into the room. It can make a dramatic difference to hang them the other way round, especially for a small room. If you do this you'll probably have to move the light switch, which can be an added expense, but it will be worth it.

A classic example of a bottom-heavy property (see plan, over) is a standard Georgian or Victorian terrace with steps up to the front door, a full-sized lower ground floor and a first floor with two rooms on it. The bathroom that was outside when the house was built has been moved to the first floor to suit modern requirements – this uses one of the two rooms on the first floor, therefore leaving only one bedroom and two floors of reception space. Such a property would benefit greatly from having a loft extension – providing an extra two bedrooms – and possibly a multiple-height rear extension to house bathrooms.

Loft conversions

Planning authorities are unlikely to allow you to raise the ridge (highest point of the roof) height of your house unless a precedent has been set with other houses in the area or if your house is very different architecturally. First go into the loft and have a good look. See how much head height you have up there already, but don't forget you will probably have to strengthen the floor, which will raise it a good 6 inches or more and thus lose you the same amount of height. If there is enough height in the loft to stand up comfortably and you have established from your market research and the quotes you have obtained from builders that the cost of converting it is

likely to be less than the amount it will add to the value of the property, then you probably should go ahead. To ensure that you end up with a tidy profit, bear the following in mind:

- Loft conversions are not cheap. Don't assume they will always add more value than they will cost. Find out if other similar properties nearby have had conversions and, if so, how this has affected their value.

- You don't always need planning permission to convert your loft. Get in touch with your local planning department for advice on what possibilities are open to you.

- Any work that affects the actual structure of the building (which basically means putting anything into the roof void, as when the property was built it is likely that the joists were not intended to do anything but hold up the ceiling below) will need building regulation approval. Again, seek advice from the building regulation department at your local council offices. It is illegal not to secure the correct building regulation approval – you may jeopardise the structural integrity of the building. Not only this but when you come to sell the property your purchaser will not have the necessary approvals required by their mortgage company. You will almost certainly lose your sale.

- You can add extra space by mansarding the existing roof slope. This means steepening the existing pitch and results in an almost flat roof coming out to meet it.

(This is a very common feature of European and US architecture). In this country they are often only permitted on the rear of a building as they dramatically change the way the building looks.

- To convert your loft into a habitable room you will need to comply with building regulations for insulation and emergency exits. This may affect other areas of the property as you must ensure there is a safe route out of the new room in case of fire. You may also have to fit a mains (not battery-powered) smoke alarm.

Extensions

Extensions have been built onto existing dwellings for as long as those dwellings themselves have been built – indeed, many of the main facades of the stately homes we now visit are themselves extensions onto smaller or differently styled houses. It has been known for an extension to be so large that the original building is pretty much swallowed up within it. At the other end of the scale, smaller changes, such as a new porch, are also classified as an extension.

Extensions are a bigger subject than loft conversions, as they involve building onto the existing dwelling to a lesser or greater degree, rather then being restricted by the existing space. In other words, the scope of what you can do is in essence unlimited, except for cost and planning permission. The reason for building any extension should be, as with all your property decisions, to reflect the requirements of the potential occupiers more precisely.

- As with loft conversions, you may not need planning permission to extend – contact your local planning department to enquire about permitted development.

- Almost all extensions will require building regulation approval.

- An extension is a good way to make an older property, that was originally designed with a different lifestyle in mind, match the requirements of today's housebuyer.

- Do not get carried away with an extension – think about why you feel you need to build one. Does the property really benefit from this costly extra?

- Make sure that you are not adding too much living space for the number of bedrooms. If your extension means your living space is no longer in balance with your bedroom space it probably won't actually add as much value as you hoped.

- In some areas, creating a sun room/conservatory can be a cheap way of adding extra living space.

Cellars

Another means of adding space to your property is by way of a cellar conversion – in the right property a cellar conversion can be a great way to add much-needed space but, as always, there is no point in spending your money unless you are going to do the job properly.

From the purchaser's point of view, one of the most important features of a cellar is adequate head height. Traditionally, cellars were used to store coal and so rarely have full head height. You can overcome this problem by digging down into the ground. Whether you do this yourself or hire a builder to do it for you, it is essential the work is always carried out in accordance with the requirements of your local building inspector. Done wrong, it can seriously affect the foundations of the building. This is not a complicated job, but it is very hard work.

If you want your cellar to be termed a habitable room you must comply with building regulations. There are no strict building regulation requirements for minimum head height in a room, but common sense will tell you that a purchaser is unlikely to be wowed by your cellar if they have to crawl around on their hands and knees. There are, however, building regulation requirements that state there must be a minimum head height of 2 metres above all stairs and landings. Your cellar must also have the correct ventilation and fire exit.

For any type of extension or conversion, remember that if you are not the freeholder of the property you will need to inform and get agreement from the freeholder as well as from the building inspector.

Architects carry huge
amounts of building
and design know-how
in their heads

Employing an architect

If you are planning any major design or architectural changes to your property you will need to think about getting an architect on board. Having both a project manager and an architect is a relatively new concept (in the last 25 years or so). Traditionally, the architect would have fulfilled both functions. This change can work well, as the role of project manager is essentially a managerial one and architects are more artistically driven.

If you are applying for planning permission to carry out a loft conversion or build an extension you will need to submit all the right forms, correctly filled out, along with all the necessary drawings, drawn accurately to scale, to your planning office. If you're not totally confident you can do this then I would suggest you employ an architect. Your average architect has trained for seven years to acquire the vast amount of knowledge needed to do the job – so don't be cocky and assume you can simply whip out a drawing and get planning permission sorted without similar knowledge. A great deal of what an architect does happens before he or she even picks up a pen. Architects carry huge amounts of building and design know-how in their heads. They generally know what you are likely to get planning permission for and, as such, are far more likely to be able to get it for you. You can waste many, many months trying to do it yourself and having your applications refused by your planning department again and again.

As with many professions, the cost of an architect can vary dramatically. To get planning permission you need scale drawings of at least 1:100 of both the existing and proposed elevations of your property. Architects charge around £55 an hour for this service (you can find a suitable architect via the Royal Institute of British Architects – RIBA). An architect who does everything from concept to project management, right up until the moment they hand the keys back to you, is likely to charge between 10 and 13% of the total cost of works for a relatively straightforward residential property. Again, personal recommendation is your number-one route to a good architect. Make sure you employ someone you can talk easily and freely to, who listens to what you have to say and who appears to understand not only where you are coming from but also how you visualise the finished property.

You are also likely to need to employ a structural surveyor if you are doing anything that affects the existing structure of the building or has any structural integrity (i.e. that is holding anything up).

Partly for insurance reasons, professionals such as structural surveyors will be employed directly by you. The architect or project manager will confer with them with regard to the property but ultimately they are working directly for you.

Extending your space

Bungalows are great properties to develop because they often have very large loft areas and are usually built on generous plots of land.

Terry Rich wasn't new to the business of property developing. He had renovated a few of his previous homes over the years and sold them for a profit. However, his previous projects had not made enough money to afford him the luxury of living elsewhere while the work was being done. Terry, his wife Sarah, and their three small children had got used to living in the middle of building chaos. Their ambition this time around, therefore, was to generate enough money to allow Terry to buy two properties, one to live in and one to develop. To achieve this, Terry would need to generate a substantial profit.

The Budget £

Terry's plan was to buy a property he could extend both upwards and outwards, and thereby secure a six-figure profit of £120,000 in just six months.

Property bought for	£159,000
Projected cost of works	£20,000
Projected selling price	£300,000
Projected gross profit	£121,000 (67.6%)

What he bought

Terry decided on a two-bed bungalow in Tonbridge that nestled in the corner of the beautiful Kent countryside.

The plan

Although the property as it stood only required a simple renovation, Terry wanted to capitalise on the views from the 130-ft southfacing garden by building a huge garden room at the back of the property. He was also set on an impressive open roof for the garden room, which would let the sun pour through. Secondly, Terry decided to convert the loft to provide two extra bedrooms, a toilet and a shower room.

My advice

I agreed with Terry and Sarah that the single-floor dwelling had a roof space just crying out for a loft conversion. I advised them to:

BE OBJECTIVE. Terry and Sarah wanted to move the existing front door and replace it with a decorative stained-glass window. The design didn't fit in with the style of the rest of the house and meant that the main entrance to the house was now straight into the kitchen. The window cost them £600, which I thought was a waste of money, but they went ahead anyway. Their design for the new window revealed how personal they were getting with the project. I advised them that

Terry and Sarah were convinced that fitting a stained-glass window at the bottom of the stairs would be a winner. In fact, their subjective approach meant they were wasting their money.

making such a personal statement might cause them problems when they came to sell. Most potential buyers would have a strong opinion one way or the other about the window.

USE SPACE ACCORDING TO YOUR MARKET. Terry rightly decided to exploit the extra space in the master bedroom on the first floor. But he fitted not an ensuite shower or bathroom but, strangely, a study. His argument was that people spend more time at a computer than in a shower. But, in fact, ensuite bathrooms constantly appear in the top ten wishlist of buyers, alongside good decoration and off-street parking.

BREAK DOWN YOUR BUDGET. Terry had calculated the cost of the work needed to cover electrics, plumbing, joinery, plastering, floors and decoration, and external works, but had not broken down his budget into itemised sections, which meant he didn't really know how much he had to spend in each area and so his budget could very easily have run away from him. Also, he'd failed to factor in any contingencies. With any project, and especially a large-scale one like Terry's, this is a major oversight. I felt that his overall budget of £20,000 was fantastically optimistic.

CHECK THE CEILING PRICE. Terry had not found out what was the highest potential selling price for a property such as his in the area. When I advised him to investigate prices by looking in the windows of nearby estate agents, he discovered that the ceiling price was actually £250,000 – £50,000 less than his projected sale price of £300,000.

On one of my visits I found that a mistake had already been made; the new exterior walls were taller than the existing walls because Terry hadn't read the plans properly. This oversight lead to an overspend of £500 in extra labour and materials.

Terry planned to leave the rafters exposed to create a greater sense of space in the extension.

As Terry was affecting the structure of the building with the roof extension the local building inspector wished to discuss this on one of his visits. Terry did not seem too pleased to see him, even though a building inspector can in fact be of immense help and support during the running of a site. Terry hadn't realised that the weight of his massive loft conversion on the existing walls and foundations would be an issue. The building inspector needed to see the size of the existing foundations under the supporting wall. So, Terry had to dig down beside his foundations to see if they were man enough for the job. If they hadn't been he would have had to spend a considerable amount of money underpinning them (strengthening them from below). This would have put even more pressure on Terry's project, when the costs

The end result was a bright and airy room. Fitting roof lights max-imised the feeling of openness and light in this space.

Changes that affect neighbouring properties

It is important to remember that your neighbours may have a say in your planning process. I would always advise you to smooth the way by talking through the project with your neighbours before putting in your application, to make sure there are no nasty surprises later on. Once you have submitted your planning application your plans are then registered with the council and your neighbours are notified and/or a notice is posted. Your neighbours then have 21 days in which to lodge an objection. If there are objections the decision may go to committee. Terry had not thought about the effect his garden room and loft would have on his neighbours. As it turned out, his neighbours did object to his application and because his loft conversion would have overlooked the neighbouring properties, he had to reduce the size of two second-floor windows, and use frosted glass in one of the windows so that their privacy wasn't invaded.

were already running away like a steam train. But he was lucky. Although he lost a week waiting, his foundations got the OK.

Final sums

Property bought for	£159,000
Final cost of works including fees	**£50,000**
Target selling price	£315,000
Target gross profit	**£106,000 (50.7%)**

Terry's original budget for the work was £20,000. In the end he overshot this by a massive £30,000. These overspends were due to the cost of labour, an unnecessary decorative window, failure to read the plans properly, trusting friends to do the work… And the list goes on.

When the work was complete, Terry wanted to put the property on the market for a whacking £315,000, which was higher than the top valuation from local estate agents. There is a real danger in doing this – you could fail to even get people through the front door. It is safer to put the property on at a reasonable price and so secure greater interest. Several interested parties may even start a lucrative (for you!) bidding war. Don't forget that the real value of your property is only as much as someone is willing to pay for it.

Terry and Sarah developed their property with a family market in mind. They correctly chose a traditional, relatively rustic kitchen that would appeal to this market.

Terry took three serious gambles with his development project: 1) that £20,000 would cover the job; 2) that he could go ahead without breaking down his costs and; 3) that he would hit his target price of £300,000 (higher than the top valuation he had received). The property did go onto the market at £315,000, but this was only because Terry felt he *had* to put it on at that figure to justify the cost of the extra work. The other two gambles had cost him a huge £30,000. At £315,000, Terry and Sarah stood to make a £106,000 profit. Not at all bad, but if he had stuck to his budget his profit would have been a fantastic £136,000! **(2001)**

Terry and Sarah were right to install a fireplace in their sitting room and create a focal point. However, the style was probably too contemporary for the house and was not to everyone's taste.

Where are they now?

Terry and Sarah eventually secured an offer for £305,000 but the buyer subsequently pulled out. They therefore took the bungalow off the market over the winter of 2001 and put it back on for £299,500 in spring 2002. They had a lot of interest and received another offer for £305,000, but just as they were due to exchange the chain broke down again. Undaunted, Terry and Sarah have boldly decided to buy another bungalow to modernise as they wait to sell their current one. Once their first bungalow has sold, they will move into rented accommodation while Terry continues with the development of the second property. **(2002)**

Getting permissions

If you have decided that you would like to do a loft conversion or extension you first need to work out whether planning permission is required and, if so, what the likelihood is you will get it. Getting permission from external bodies is not something you are able to control so it can make your project take longer to get off the ground and therefore cost you more money than you had hoped.

Play by the rules

Assuming the property is not listed or in a conservation area (see page 92), you are generally entitled to permitted development rights, which will allow you to extend your property by 50–70 cubic metres, as long as this allowance has not already been used up by previous owners. This extension therefore requires only building regulation approval, not planning permission.

If you attempt to bypass any of the planning procedures, in an attempt to avoid the time and effort involved in submitting applications, you will not only have problems selling (as your buyer's solicitor will ask for documentary evidence of building approval) but you might end up in court. The legal requirements that you might need include:

- Planning permission

- Building regulation approval

- Conservation areas consent and listed building consent

- Landlord's consent

- Party wall agreements

- Highways licence (for materials or a skip stored on the roadside)

Planning permission

This is required when the work you plan to do is not within your permitted development rights.

Each council will have its own policy that will have been agreed with the government to suit the local area. Planning permission is generally granted if the application falls within this policy. You can buy a copy of a document called the 'local plan' from your local planning department, which sets out its policy. This will tell you whether you are likely to require planning permission and, if so, whether you are likely to get it (you might want to rope in your surveyor or architect to help you out with the jargon!). Experience, again, will serve you well. Different councils have different priorities and once you become familiar with your local planning department you will quickly learn what you can and can't do in each area. If you do need planning permission you'll need to get the application forms from the planning office and then provide detailed 1:100 drawings (or get your architect to do so). An example of a planning application form can be found in Appendix 3 (see pages 155 to 157), though you should note that the style of the form does differ according to the council involved. Most councils will have a facility for you to download the form direct from their website.

A planning application is not dissimilar to a legal case – it is based on current policy and case studies of previously approved and refused applications. Someone who is dealing with the local council regularly will be familiar with all of this and so is more likely to submit an application that will be approved. If you are not familiar, and either do not word your application correctly or submit too little detail, you may find yourself going backwards and forwards with application after application for a long time before you get an approval.

With both planning permission and building regulations there is nothing to stop you commencing the work before you actually have approval but you do so entirely at your own risk. If the alterations are not approved you will, at your own cost, have to undo your work and redo it in accordance with the stipulations of the planning department or, even worse, reinstate what was originally there. The planning department has the right to legally enforce these requirements, so there's no way out. In any case, if you have not resolved these issues you are unlikely to ever be able to sell the property. This is because when you come to sell you have to sign a 'seller's property information form', a copy of which you'll find in Appendix 4 (see pages 158 to 165). On this form you must detail any work you have done and sign accordingly. This is legally binding. If you don't have the necessary permissions any half-decent solicitor or mortgage company will pick up on it and will almost certainly advise the buyer they are representing not to go ahead with the sale.

Building regulations

Building regulations are very often required, even where planning permission is not – building regulations are more about how a building stays up, whether it is insulated sufficiently and whether it is safe to live in; whereas planning permission is more about how the property looks and how it affects the local area.

There are two levels of building regulation application – the building notice and the full plans application. Both are obtained from your planning office.

Building notice will be required if you are doing only minor work and the issues involved are fairly simple (e.g. moving a bathroom). The building notice informs your local building inspector that you are doing the work, who then visits the site to check that he or she is happy that you are complying with the regulations.

A full plans application will be needed for major work (e.g. a large extension). Your local building inspector will require you to send copies of your working plans in advance of your work to ensure that the building will be structurally sound, has appropriate means of escape in the event of fire and complies with all other regulations. There is also a mid-level of works where you may or may not submit a full plans application. Examples would be knocking down a structural wall or moving a chimneybreast. With this level of work my advice would be to submit the full plans application anyway, as then everyone will be clear what is required and you will avoid having to redo any work.

With all types, once you have submitted your application your local building inspector will call round periodically to check that the works are progressing in accordance with current building regulations.

For any work that affects the structure you may also be required to employ a structural engineer to assess the load bearing on certain areas. If the building control officer at the planning department is in agreement with your structural engineer's assessment you can go ahead with your work.

Conservation areas and listed buildings

Conservation areas and listed buildings have these titles because they are considered to be rather nice and of architectural and historical importance and, therefore, a dim view is taken of dramatic changes to them, unless these changes are considered to be of a high quality of design. While investing in a listed building can make property development more complicated, it can also give you a premium in value when it comes to sell.

It is important to find out whether your property is in a conservation area or is listed before you buy it, as this will affect what you are able to do to it. In both cases you will need to apply for consent for any external changes to the property (even if you are reinstalling original features or replacing like for like). Depending on the listing grade, you may also need to apply for permission to change almost anything to do with the property. Check with your local conservation officer, based at the local planning department, as to whether you need approval or not.

Conservationists will all tend to differ in opinion, so there are very few rules as to what will or will not be permitted. If a building has evolved considerably from its original state some conservation officers may not consider it to be in the best interests of the building to install pastiche original features.

Landlord's consent

If you have purchased a lease rather than the freehold of the property, the terms of the lease will generally not allow you to do certain types of works to your property. If your lease is to this effect, you will need to ask the freeholder (or landlord) for permission to carry out the work. Depending on the particular whims of your landlord this can either be a quick and relatively pain-free process or (more often) take an

Investing in a listed building can give you a premium in value when it comes to sell

inordinately long time and be pretty expensive. Plus after all that, you may not end up with your landlord's consent. Therefore, if the work is essential to making your development work, and to achieving your 20% profit, you must try to get this permission before you exchange contracts.

This is particularly relevant when it comes to developing flats. A common mistake made by buyers is to think that it is within their rights to remove carpets and sand the floorboards. In fact, many leases forbid this and going ahead could cause you difficulties when you come to sell.

Party wall agreement

This is required when you live in a terraced or semi-detached house or flat and the work you are planning to do materially affects a wall that you share with a neighbour. You will need to instruct a surveyor (at your cost) to inspect both yours and your neighbour's property to confirm the current condition of each. A letter of agreement is then signed by each party. This letter serves as an insurance to your neighbour that you are responsible for repairing any damage caused by the work you carry out. The district surveyor can shut your site down instantly if he or she discovers you do not have a party wall agreement.

Highways licence

You will need this if you are planning to put a skip or delivered materials onto the road or pavement outside your property. Often skip companies will take care of this paperwork for you but you need to check they have done so as you can be heavily fined if you do not have the correct licence. It is also your responsibility to light the skip if it is going to be there during the hours of darkness.

5

SPENDING YOUR BUDGET CORRECTLY — THE DETAIL

Deciding on the style of how you are going to arrange your interior and sticking to it is absolutely essential when developing a property. Your aim should be to keep a consistent theme throughout, that draws all the rooms and other spaces together, otherwise it will feel disjointed and unconsidered. I'm not just talking about painting the walls cream and whacking a carpet down (though neither should you be thrown by the often complicated talk of interior designers – achieving a cohesive look still comes down to a good design eye and a little basic common sense).

Harmonising your interior

A good way to help you decide on the look of your property is to find out how you feel about other people's. Start by looking at the spaces in shops, bars and restaurants, other people's homes, even offices. Examine your own reaction to the different interiors. Which ones make you feel calm and tempted to sit down and linger there? Which ones make you want to run out of the door?

Choosing an overall scheme

Generally speaking, interiors that draw you in and make you feel at ease have some consistency in the choice of colours, products and materials used. Consider carefully the different colours in your property as you move from room to room. Do they make you feel relaxed and welcome or do they jolt you from one mood to another? If the latter you will need to bring some harmony into the interior scheme. This does not mean painting every wall in the exact same colour, but it does mean working to a limited number of colour ranges.

Then think about which different textures and materials will best complement the colour scheme. Current trends in interior design favour the use of a number of different textures, all based on the same colour palette. This can be very effective and produces a tactile and comfortable feeling in a property. Avoid having any particular room or area that jumps out at you as you look around the room, unless you have thought very carefully about making it a 'wow! factor' (see opposite) and it is the effect you are setting out to create. For more advice on colour see pages 112 to 113.

Once you've chosen your colour scheme and materials, and as work proceeds on any major changes to the property, you'll need to make sure you have ordered your kitchen and bathroom and have begun to source everything else. Look at the list of items you have agreed to supply on your Specification (see page 64) and check that you have decided on and ordered every single one. If the site is held up by something that is your fault (you've overlooked an order, or keep changing your mind about what you want) then you've no right to pressure others into keeping to the timetable.

It's important not to confuse the wow! factor with the 'truly bizarre' factor

The kitchen

Received wisdom says that an amazing kitchen can almost sell a property in itself. It can. But not at the expense of the rest of the property. Every room must be right and you must spread your budget accordingly. Splashing out 90% of your budget on the kitchen will not get you the top price for your property.

Kitchens can broadly be split up into a) kitchen/breakfast rooms b) galley kitchens and c) living-room kitchens. There are certain design guidelines that apply to all and others that are particularly relevant to either a), b) or c). The following pointers should help you identify which kitchen you should go for, what the major design considerations are for each type, and how much money you should be spending.

The importance of a wow! factor

With so much competition out there it is really important to add that little extra to your property and create the all-important wow! factor. It does mean spending a bit more but it will pay off, as your property will be the one to stand out. If prospective buyers have been trawling around 20-odd homes, yours is the one they will remember. So bearing your market in mind, think carefully about what would make your property a cut above the rest. A beautiful fireplace is an obvious choice, as are garden features such as a pergola or great lighting, a wet room, an amazing kitchen or a stunning staircase. The wow! will often be one particular room or in the garden, but it can be anywhere, as long as it produces the desired reaction (try it out on friends first!). If someone feels this way about the property there is a good chance they will simply have to own it. It's important not to confuse the wow! factor with the 'truly bizarre' factor. As with the rest of the property, you still need to avoid getting too carried away with your own eccentric tastes that may only appeal to a limited number of like-minded buyers, so avoid Egyptian thrones for lavatories or scarlet wall tiles.

 ## Designing your kitchen – all types

The basic rules of kitchen design, together with appropriate use of materials and colour, apply to any type of kitchen space, for any market. When planning your kitchen start by looking at where the soil pipe is positioned on the outside of the building as it is cheaper and easier to have your sink, dishwasher and washing machine near to this pipe. Plan your kitchen around that area, bearing in mind the sight lines when you walk into the kitchen and from different positions. To create a beautiful kitchen you don't need to order a bespoke model, just use your imagination and think practically. If you feel unsure where to start, consider the following points. They are relevant to all kitchens. And remember, once you've decided on your kitchen, place your order – some kitchens can take over eight weeks to be delivered and you don't want your site to be held up and your profit to dwindle while you're waiting for your units to arrive.

- Think about how you actually *use* a kitchen and choose your items of furniture/fittings accordingly.

- Don't feel you need to stuff the whole kitchen with units. If you are careful with your design, and have units in one area only, you can create a kitchen/breakfast room out of a fairly small space.

- It is nice to look out of a window as you wash up. Above a sink you cannot have normal-height units anyway, as you would hit your head, so this is a logical place not to have any wall units.

- Have a worktop either side of the sink so you can put things down.

- Using different materials for different areas of worktop can help designate space for different uses.

- Avoid a design that forces you to walk miles from the fridge to the hob. Generally things come out of the fridge, onto the cooker and then move to the sink, so keep it user-friendly.

- Ovens and extractors generally look best with symmetrical units either side, making them a focal feature of the room. With current styles extractors and cookers are designed to look really stunning as well as functional.

- Don't forget that a full-height fridge or a fridge-freezer is very bulky, so try to design your kitchen so your fridge can stand against two walls (see diagram, opposite). Otherwise it tends to be a big lump at the end of a run of units.

Pulling one colour or material from the splashback and taking it through to the flooring is a good way of creating cohesion

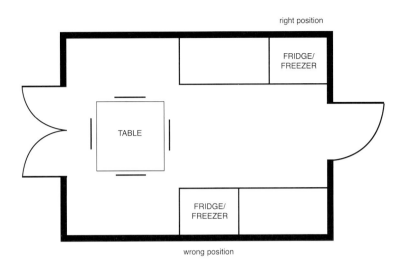

right position

FRIDGE/
FREEZER

TABLE

FRIDGE/
FREEZER

wrong position

Giving your kitchen a cohesive feel – all types

All the different elements of a kitchen need to flow and be consistent – the flooring, worktop, splashback and units must all be considered together. Too many different materials or colours and the kitchen will look as though no thought has been put into it. If you have decided to use wood-effect doors, a popular choice for any room, bear in mind that the flooring should either match exactly or be totally different. A halfway solution will just look wrong – and cheap. Equally, the carcass of units must not jar with either the door or flooring. Stick to a theme for materials and colours; for example, cream and black or chrome, yellow and grey. Pulling one colour or material from the splashback and taking it through to the flooring is a good way of creating cohesion.

The kitchen/breakfast room

In a perfect world, with no space or cost limitations, almost every kitchen would be a kitchen/breakfast room. The way we live today increasingly requires a kitchen to be multifunctional. With some exceptions, different members of the household no longer cook and eat at separate sittings, as in Victorian times. The kitchen/breakfast room is where people come together to cook, eat and chat and so they require a room large enough to accommodate all these activities. The trend in creating extensions to Victorian terraces, either at the end of the kitchen or by filling in the side return, to house the kitchen/breakfast room shows the importance people place on this space. The kitchen should strike a good balance between style and comfort. It needs to be welcoming, with enough room for a table and chairs, but also pleasing to the eye, as a lot of time will be spent in it. It is, after all, the room that on a day-to-day basis takes the brunt of our chaotic lives.

Galley kitchens/small kitchens

Sometimes, particularly in flats, space restrictions mean you simply won't be able to create a kitchen/breakfast room. If you have a small or galley kitchen then all is not lost. Just because it is small this doesn't mean it has to be a horrible pokey hole. There are lots of ways you can make a kitchen with restricted space more appealing. A galley kitchen can look amazing but you need to concentrate much more on the detailing and design. The following tips will help you make the most of a small kitchen space.

- Open up part of the wall, even if it's only down to worktop height, to enable you to see into the living room. Fit shutters or folding doors so you have the choice of whether or not to look into the other room. And from the living room's point of view, having the option of shutting yourself off is always handy, especially if your kitchen has a tendency to look a mess!

- Use narrower wall units as base units on one side of the room as they are much more shallow (300-mm rather than 600-mm deep). This will give a similar visual effect and provide storage and work space.

- Check out different-shaped sinks – you don't have to go for the standard shape and there are some alternative designs that look much more comfortable in smaller kitchens. Bowl sinks are popular at the moment and have plenty of space around them.

- Think about putting the washing machine elsewhere (in a cupboard, the bathroom, the cellar).

With a galley kitchen the detail of the design is of the utmost importance because anyone looking at it with a view to buy will be right up close, not viewing it from a distance. If you have space for only a few units make sure they are of top quality and design – getting the best units won't cost much more relatively speaking, as the overall number of units is low.

Beat the competition

A kitchen is not only a major expense but to change it is a major disruption. The kitchen you fit must therefore appeal to a wide market both now and in the future. If in doubt keep it very simple and plain – if you really must make a statement do it with the wall colour or the splashbacks so that if your purchaser does take offence it can be changed very easily and cheaply.

The living-room kitchen

Housing your kitchen in the living room is also fashionable at the moment – particularly in modern, open-plan apartments. This is because this organisation of space precisely suits how many young professionals want to live their lives today, with one big room housing all their living requirements, rather than several separate, smaller rooms. If you are developing a modern property with cutting-edge design, because you know that there is a substantial local market for this type of property, then a living-room kitchen could be a very good move. Remember, you'll need a really superb finish and must make the kitchen design consistent with the rest of the property. An ultra-modern space with a kitchen that isn't ultra-modern is simply a disaster. However, bear in mind that with this type of design you are likely to cut off the majority of families, sharers and other market categories.

Get ahead	In some properties it can be acceptable to leave spaces for the washing machine and fridge rather than putting them in, thereby saving you money. Check with your estate agent as to what you potential buyer is likely to expect.

How much should you spend on your kitchen?

In terms of your kitchen budget, the most important thing is that you don't over or underspend for the type of property you are developing. Underspending on an expensive property can leave you with no sale where as overspending can not only look bizarre but is also a waste of your money. There really are better things to do with it, so bear in mind all the fun things you could do with the extra money if you feel tempted to overspend.

Agas can look amazing – but only in the right property. You may dream of living in a farmhouse in the Cotswolds but if the property you are actually selling is a suburban terrace with a galley kitchen then forget the Aga – it just won't go and you shouldn't try to fight it. Always match your kitchen to your potential market and the size and style of your property. A galley kitchen in a 6-bedroomed house will be a problem, just as it is ridiculous to have a fabulous bespoke hand-crafted oak number in a tiny basement flat. There are no official figures as to how much you should spend on your kitchen (despite what some kitchen salesmen might tell you) but it must look right – browse through magazines for pictures of kitchens in similar properties or ask for advice from your local estate agent.

Kitchens for rental properties

If you are *selling* the property the new occupants will have paid thousands of pounds of their lifetime savings in order to secure the purchase and therefore have an active interest in keeping everything looking in tip-top condition. With renters, this logic does not apply, so avoid shiny laminate that can scratch and wood-block that needs regular oiling. Keep different colours to a minimum so that it is easier to redecorate – choose appropriate colours for the property but keep it simple so that you appeal to as broad a market as possible. Most renters will expect a fridge and washing machine as standard and in some properties a dishwasher, tumble dryer and microwave may be essential. Check with your local letting agent for advice. For most 6–12 month lets I'd advise you to avoid providing cutlery, pots and pans or plates, as the tenants would rather provide their own (after all, these are relatively cheap items for them to buy). Remember, there's no need to put in what is not required – it just means more to break and more to replace.

Sourcing your kitchen

When looking to buy a kitchen it's a good idea to really hunt around, as there are lots of options out there. Many kitchen suppliers will be able to supply you with a 3D printout showing how your new kitchen will look and this can be very helpful with your planning. Remember to measure the room carefully (including doors and windows) before heading off to the showroom. Be aware that most kitchens in showrooms have very expensive worktops, lighting, cornicing, pelmets and splashbacks that are NOT included as part of the kitchen. In order to assess whether the kitchen you have your eye on really is right, therefore, you'll need to visually strip away these items, which represent a great deal of the cost of a kitchen. Check out the carcasses of the units by opening the doors and drawers. This can be the area in which a kitchen that looks fine at first glance falls down on closer inspection.

Beat the competition	Using oversized furniture can make any room feel smaller than it actually is. Avoid a king-size four-poster bed in a normal-sized bedroom. In smaller bathrooms source smaller cabinets/baths/loos and in the kitchen use smaller units and fewer of them. Keep ornaments and other accessories to a minimum or it will feel like you are trying to squash lots of things into a small space.

The living room

This must be a comfortable and welcoming space that is consistent with the rest of the property and which reflects the lifestyle of the prospective buyer. It is one of the few rooms in a property that has not changed a great deal in terms of its use and requirements over the last hundred years.

The importance of light

When it comes to the living room, one of the things that really attracts buyers is good light. The amount of light coming in to a space is important with any room, but especially with the living area. Sunshine will pour in (well, in theory) to your living room at a certain time during the day, depending on the direction in which your property faces. Bear this in mind when deciding what colours to paint the walls. If your living room only receives strong natural light for a limited period of the day then compensate for this by using bright colours such as white, cream or yellow. Other great tips for increasing the amount of light, both artificial and natural are:

• Use cleverly placed artificial directional lights – these can create an amazing impression in a room that with normal ceiling lights alone could look dark.

• Fit a false window glazed with sandblasted glass to the wall and high voltage lights behind. When the lights are switched on this will give the impression of an external window. This is particularly effective in rooms that are modern in design and can make an amazing focal feature.

• Use light-coloured curtains in floaty fabrics if these fit the design of the room.

Uniting new with old

Many of us live in houses and flats built over 100 years ago, yet the objects within them are very much of the present. It can be tricky to accommodate the amount of modern technology typically found in any home – TV, DVD, sound system and speakers, computer – into a traditional interior. Depending on the type of property, it may be appropriate to fit wires for a centrally controlled system when re-wiring – we are moving forward fast though, so make sure that what you consider to be cutting edge technology now still is when you actually want to fit it. The secret is to ensure modern technology, and especially the wires needed to run it, are discreet. And try to keep a balance in the room by maintaining symmetry in the positioning of modern items.

Putting back original features – the fireplace

With older-style properties the clean fuss-free lines that were desirable in the 1970s have been forgotten and today the trend tends to be towards putting back original features, or enhancing and making a focal point of them if they are already there. And the living room is where people will expect to see period features in abundance. For most markets, in the majority of properties that predate 1920, you are most likely to maximise your profit by reinstating as many of the original features as possible. Your choice of features must be spot on – features not right for the original design of the property will stick out like a sore thumb. The fireplace is still the feature that seems to score most points with buyers. Understandably so, an appropriate fireplace can look magnificent and transform the feel of a room.

Shortly after it became fashionable to put Victorian features back into a property, fireplaces that had been removed in earlier decades all came out of the woodwork (or people's garden sheds). They were plentiful and relatively cheap; even as recently as ten years ago you could pick up an old fireplace from a reclamation yard for £30. But their popularity and a finite supply drove prices up and now a reproduction and an original differ very little in price. Make sure you put the right fireplace, of the right size, in the right room. Don't be tempted to save money and fit a tiny bedroom fireplace into a large chimneybreast in the living room – it can look absurd.

Fashions for fireplaces and fire surrounds change fast. Now that in most homes fireplaces are primarily a decorative feature, with their original use as a source of heat relegated to second place, the imagination has been able to run riot. Even though times have changed, many households still feel a certain nostalgia for the days when families gathered round an open fire. While few families will actually do this, they still enjoy the image the fireplace conjures up. An alternative to an original fireplace is to create a hole in the wall and have a freestanding grate perhaps with traditional surround. This is not a particularly efficient fire in terms of heat but if heat is not what you are looking for it can create a great focal point for the room.

The imitation coal and log fires that began to appear around 1930 marked a breakthrough – people no longer had to lug around coal and wood and clean out fires, as they had been doing for hundreds of years. These too seem to have had their heyday although high-quality gas fires can still look great in the right property. If your market is older people, or inner-city dwellers for whom it is either illegal or just plain impractical to have a real fire, coal-effect fires can be a great choice.

The living room is where people will most expect to see period features in abundance

→ Other period features

CORNICING AND DECORATIVE PLASTERWORK

Estate agents' details will highlight period features, due to their popularity. Cornicing, dado rails and other decorative elements can help secure a sale on your property, but you must avoid being tempted by cheap replicas. Look up 'Plastering' in your *Yellow Pages* and find a decorative plasterer – it's more expensive but really worth it. Make sure cornicing and coving is fitted well because if you are aware of the joints it can simply defeat the object.

DOORS

Stripping the paint off doors has been a fashionable pastime for the last 20 years or so. While I am not saying you should not strip your doors and woodwork, you should make sure you do so in full knowledge of all the facts:

• It is not necessarily a cheaper or easier job than painting.

• Most doors made in Victorian times were mass produced from soft wood and always intended to be painted, so you are unlikely to ever get a beautiful finish – however much you sand and wax them!

• If you're sending your doors away to be stripped there are both practical and time considerations to be taken into account (see box, below).

Stripping doors

The process of sending your doors away to be stripped involves dipping them in a massive bath of sodium hydroxide, which thoroughly soaks the door. It can take months for the doors to properly dry out, so repainting is heavily delayed. The process also tends to cause the wood to warp and split and, as it dissolves the organic glue, it can cause the joints to ease apart. I have no doubt that in 20 years' time there will be people cursing those of us (myself included) who have had van loads of doors sent away to be dipped. The fashions will have moved on and we'll be trying to create a perfect paint finish on wonky, warped and split doors. Having said that, if the previous owner was someone with a penchant for applying gloss paint in large quantities, allowing thick rivers of drips to dry all over woodwork, you may find that manually stripping or burning the paint off might actually prove easier in the long run, even if you are planning on repainting it.

The bathroom

Your bathroom must have a practical as well as aesthetic appeal. It is a haven where the distractions that are part of the rest of the house (phone, TV, music) have no place. And a hot bath is one of the best forms of relaxation ever invented.

A history

Sophisticated drainage was in existence before the Romans were around, but in this country flushing loos in every home did not become the norm until 1778, when merchants, including Mr Thomas Crapper, mass marketed the water closet (WC). Today the bathroom is, with the kitchen, arguably one of the most important rooms in the house when it comes to making or breaking a sale. Prior to lavatory factories and the advent of Victorian drainage, there would have been a nightly cart collecting human waste from each household to be dumped in the river. Not surprisingly, having a flushing loo was seen as the height of luxury. WCs were generally located outside the property as this was considered more hygienic, was simple and cheap to plumb and kept unpleasant smells away from the interior.

Market requirements

When planning and designing your bath, always think of it not simply as a room housing a bath, loo and basin but also as a space that offers a simple yet luxurious setting for your bathing experience. Personally I spend hours in the bathroom at a time. For many people, bath-time is also an important family occasion when everyone can be together, perhaps even more so than for mealtimes in the kitchen. Being a bath person, I find it difficult to understand why the majority of the population actually likes showers, but I do understand that a shower is an essential time-saving feature that will be demanded and expected by many buyers. Therefore, you should try to, as a minimum requirement, fit a shower door onto your bath and a bath-shower mixer with hook above. The 'power shower' that has become fashionable in the last five to ten years is achieved by fitting a pump to the water supply to the shower – this is not feasible with all types of boiler systems, especially combinations (see pages 109 to 110). So if you feel that a power shower is an essential extra for your particular market, check with your plumber before deciding on which heating system you should use.

As always, keep the expectations of your market in mind. Do not be tempted to get carried away with YOUR dream bathroom – we all love the flake advert, that's why they made it, but recreating such a bathroom will cost a lot of money and simply won't look right in a terraced house.

Designing a bathroom – practical considerations

When planning a bathroom layout first locate the 4-inch (110-mm) soil and vent pipe than runs outside the property. From your loo you need to run another 4-inch pipe to join into this down pipe with a fall of at least 14 mm per 1 m. Therefore, the closer you position the loo to this soil pipe the cheaper and easier the plumbing of your bathroom will be and the less boxing you will need. Occasionally you may have enough space in the void under the floorboards in which to run this pipe, but it must run in the same direction as the joists (i.e. the opposite way to the floorboards) or you'll have to cut though the joists, which will make the floor collapse!

The alternative is to fit a macerator, which chomps up the waste matter that goes down the loo and can pump it away down a pipe as small as $1^1/_2$ inches in diameter to join the soil pipe. The only drawback with macerators are that a) they make a noise b) they are more prone to become blocked and you are more limited as to the items you can put down them and c) it's another machine that can go wrong. However, if you cannot locate the loo near the soil pipe, a macerator can be the only solution.

Don't forget that for all newly located bathrooms you must get building regulation approval. One requirement stipulated by the regulations is that you have an extractor fan wired into the light switch. If you are merely replacing an existing bathroom, easy ways of keeping the costs down are to use the existing pan and just replace the cistern, loo seat and flush handle, and change only the taps, splashbacks and flooring.

Beat the competition

However small your flat or house, if you can fit a bath in, then do. Not everyone likes showers and you'll be narrowing your range of buyers considerably if a shower is all you can offer. Of course, the ideal situation is to have both, even if it's only a shower attachment.

Wet rooms

These are a fantastic feature, especially in properties that have limited space. Wet rooms are very popular and are common in modern developments and loft-style apartments. A wet room means effectively turning the whole room into a shower by tiling the entire floor area on a slight slope so the water runs towards a drain hole. This can either be done by graduating the floor or by gradually increasing the amount of tile adhesive you use as you move away from the drain. I would not advise you to do this yourself but if you do want to have a go then don't forget your spirit level! Wet rooms not only look amazing, they can make a small shower room look bigger and can be that all-important wow! factor that clinches a sale (see box, page 97). Make sure you seal the corners of the room well with silicone as there are several different points through which the water can leak to the floor below.

The lure of the ensuite

We have come a long way since the time, at the turn of the last century, when having one entire room dedicated to washing was considered almost decadent. Fashions have moved hand-in-hand with advances in technology – having a bath and basin in one room and a loo in another is still common in some homes, but an ensuite is not really considered a luxury anymore. Indeed, many people expect it. You can create a second bathroom even if you are very short of space, as long as it is big enough for a loo, basin and shower; although if you can fit in a bath as well as a shower this is preferable. Ideally the master bedroom should have an ensuite, and with additional bedrooms the ratio of bedrooms to bathrooms should be no more than 3:1, otherwise the property will feel unbalanced.

The downstairs loo

This is a room that many buyers will really appreciate, especially when there is a low bathroom-to-bedroom ratio, or in a family house where there are likely to be children. If the space is big enough to house a cloakroom too, so much the better.

The outside loo, a leftover from when the house was originally built, is usually best removed, as it can make the property seem out-of-date. However, if it doesn't have a detrimental effect on the design of the kitchen or the property as a whole, then there's no reason it not to keep it (plus it's ideal for the occasional barbecue). If you do decide to remove it, you can either retain the building as a useful garden shed or demolish it, depending on where it sits in relation to the rest of the building and the garden.

How much should you spend on your bathroom?

You can pick up a new bathroom suite for as little as £150 but don't forget that a large part of your budget for a new bathroom will be swallowed up by the fitting and plumbing. While there is no point in skimping on the look of a bathroom, neither is there any need to spend a fortune; you can create an amazing effect with careful design. Splashbacks in a bathroom have more impact than the suite itself, so if you have a little bit of your budget to spare, spend it on the splashbacks. The bathroom is one of the only rooms where you can get away with not having an external window. Ensure you have good extraction though, otherwise condensation can be a problem.

➲ Bathrooms in rental properties

Tenants will usually take less care of any property than homeowners – cleanliness is not always next to godliness in their minds – and you need to adjust your approach to bathroom design accordingly. The following tips will save you work and money.

• Fit a good shower screen in the bathroom, extractor fans on a long over-run and plenty of splashbacks.

• Avoid lots of small tiles. Tile grout and silicone will start to look grey after a couple of years and regrouting is a job I wouldn't wish on my worst enemy. Good alternatives for rental properties are large sheets of toughened glass or larger tiles with fewer grout lines.

• To clean up tiles try pouring thick (uncoloured) bleach from the top of the tiles and letting it drip down. Leave for a few hours and rinse off. Then use a sharp blade to cut out the silicone before reapplying.

• If your tenants have been extremely neglectful, or you are extremely busy, call in industrial cleaners (who can restore even the most disgusting oven to something close to its former glory), ready for the new tenants.

➲ Boilers, hot water and heating systems – the options

This is an area in which a great deal of knowledge is still not enough. You can find specialist heating designers quite easily but each is likely to have a different view on your heating requirements and, of course, they cost money. Basically the choice is between a mains-fed or cold-water storage system. Whichever system you end up going for, all boilers need flue outlets at least 600 mm from an opening window.

MAINS FED

If you choose a mains-fed system, you can either have a combination boiler or an unvented hot-water cylinder. Both systems negate the need for a cold-water storage tank, so a mains-fed system is a good option if space is at a premium.

COMBINATION BOILERS

In smaller properties these are fantastic and have been used extensively in the UK over the last 15 years or so. The boiler heats water directly from the mains as you use it. It is limited as to the amount of water it can heat up at the same and so is best for smaller properties where there's only one bathroom and no excessive demand for water. You are unlikely to get a powerful shower with a combination boiler and with this type of system a separate electric shower is often fitted to heat cold water independently from the boiler. You can get combination boilers that store a small amount of hot water inside them but these are about the same size as a fridge and again need to be situated on an outside wall. This type of combination boiler is ideal if the demand for water is greater than can be provided for by a standard combination boiler.

UNVENTED HOT-WATER CYLINDERS

With this system you will require a boiler and a hot-water cylinder but still do not need a cold-water storage tank. The unvented hot-water cylinder is appropriate if you have a number of bathrooms or are likely to want to use hot water in different locations at the same time. This is because it is able to store the heated water. You will need building regulation approval to change any of these systems. Unlike combination boilers, which are limited by the capacity of the boiler, unvented hot-water cylinders are limited by the capacity of the boiler *and* the mains pressure. You may need to upgrade the size of your incoming mains for this system to work most efficiently. This can be expensive, although some water companies will give you a free lead replacement of the mains supply if you are removing lead work within the property and replacing it with 25-mm pipework. If you pay a little extra you can get a larger pipe fitted.

COLD-WATER STORAGE

This is the conventional method of heating water, ideal when there are several outlets requiring water simultaneously. There are many different types of boiler available, including the eco-friendly condensing boiler, but remember that for all types you will need space for the cold-water storage tank, hot-water cylinder and boiler (the cold-water storage tank must be situated higher than the hot-water cylinder so the water can fall). The mains fill up the cold-water storage tank until the ball cock (similar to that in a loo cistern) stops it. When you run a tap the water comes from the hot-water cylinder and the cylinder is then refilled from the cold-water storage tank, while the mains refill the cold-water storage tank. The water is heated up ready to be used when you next turn on the tap.

Hot-water cylinders are either directly or indirectly heated. Directly heated cylinders are heated with an immersion, which is a metal rod inserted into the cylinder and which is heated up by electricity (like a kettle). Indirectly heated cylinders are heated by a hollow metal coil that is placed inside the cylinder when it is made. Hot water is heated in the boiler and sent through this coil that then heats the water around it. The efficiency of the system depends on a) the capacity of the boiler to heat the water b) the size of the coil and c) the size of the pipework running around the property. For a little more money you can buy a quick recovery cylinder. This has more coils and so heats the water more quickly, so that, for example, if you use all the hot water by having six baths at the same time the water will get hot again much more quickly. With a cold-water storage system you can fit a pump on the pipework from the hot-water storage tank to a shower, which will make the water come through more quickly, so providing you with a 'power shower'. You will also want to ensure that you run the kitchen cold tap off the mains and not from the cold-water storage tank, as the cold water from the tank will have been sitting there for a while and is unsuitable for drinking.

If you've managed to take all this in – firstly, well done and secondly, have a chat to your plumber about the best boiler for your size of property. Your plumber will also be able to work out how many radiators you need and what size they need to be.

The bedroom

This room must be first and foremost a sanctuary, somewhere to escape from the hectic world outside (and maybe the hectic world inside) and curl up with a good book or magazine. Somewhere that is peaceful, welcoming, and with the minimum of clutter.

The importance of storage

When your prospective buyer walks into a bedroom you want them to be filled with a sense of calm. This cannot possibly happen if there are clothes, shoes, books, papers, magazines, CDs and other personal effects taking over the space. Therefore for the bedroom, storage is key.

It is not true to say that you can never have enough storage. You can. Too much storage will destroy the sense of balance in a room. The key is to have the right amount and type of storage, in the right place. Think about how you would like to live in the property and what storage you would need. Consider who you are marketing the property towards. For example, if there's one master-bedroom and two or three smaller rooms this will work well for families with children. If you're marketing the property to renters, bear in mind you really do need to have enough space for a wardrobe in each room.

With awkward spaces, especially in a bedroom, it is essential to install fitted wardrobes – if they are not fitted the impression will be that they have just been plonked in the room and don't really know what their function is there. With larger, squarer bedrooms, however, freestanding wardrobes are a good option as they will give you the flexibility to arrange the room however you choose. Remember that somewhere in the property you will also need to provide storage for utility items like ironing board, broom, mop and bucket and vacuum cleaner. Ensure that at least one bedroom has a wardrobe – there must be enough storage to allow the new purchaser to move in, unpack and relax all in the one day. After all, that is what they are paying you for – an easy life.

Beat the competition

While a bedroom is in real terms no different from a living room i.e. it is an empty space, you can transform the look and feel of a bedroom by having beautiful furniture rather than spending a fortune on curtains and wallpaper.

Colours and how to choose them

As you walk through the property from room to room, including corridors and other communal areas, does it feel calm and natural or does it feel like a paint colour chart? Think carefully about each room – it may look great on the paint chart but trust me, all-over purple will send a large portion of your potential market straight back out the front door. If in doubt, stick to neutrals and avoid anything that someone could feel strongly about.

Painting walls and woodwork

If you are finding it difficult to decide on your colour scheme, the solution is tester pots – definitely not a waste of money. I find that a large pile of A4-size pieces of hardboard (which you can get cut for you at any timber merchant that cuts wood) is very useful when trying out sample shades (remember to write the code on the back!). Using hardboard pieces enables you to hold up different colours together for comparison and to view the colours in different lights.

If you are aiming for a very contemporary look, old and uneven walls are simply not acceptable, so before you even choose your wall colour consider whether you need to hack off all the plaster and start again. Alternatively, accept what you have and sand and fill till you drop, then use a high-grade lining paper to give an almost smooth finish. I would recommend a slightly stronger colour in this instance, as it will be more forgiving of the uneven surface.

Often underestimated is the impact that ceiling and woodwork colours have on the wall colour. Woodwork and ceilings do not HAVE to be white and you can change the feel of a room by using alternative colours. For example, a darker ceiling will appear to reduce the height of the room, making it feel more cosy, while using the same colour on the ceiling as on the walls will blend everything together.

Currently it is fashionable to accentuate one wall with either wallpaper or by painting it in a different colour, generally darker to that used on the other walls. This means that your eye is automatically drawn to the darker wall, and if that is the main impression of the room you want people to have, it can be an effective approach. There are really no rules as to what colours you can and cannot have in a particular room, just remember not to get carried away – if there's a chance your purchaser might hate it don't do it.

Beat the competition

Integrity in your work is of paramount importance. Poor workmanship with a poor finish will jeopardise your chances of achieving the premium price you have identified in your budget. Worse still, you may end up with no profit at all. If you can't do it well yourself – get someone else to do it – you can't afford not to.

Woodwork and ceilings
do not HAVE
to be white

You can add interest to a neutral scheme by focusing on the floor covering. For years our taste in carpets have become progressively more plain and simple – the objective was to create an unobtrusive apology for a floor covering – but now we have started to explore different textures. This can enhance the appeal of your property but if you want to make your great design statement with the floor covering bear in mind that it's a great deal more expensive for the next owner to re-carpet than to repaint four walls if they don't particularly like it.

Working from home

The phenomenon of working from home has been one of the great lifestyle changes of the past 10 years or so. As a property developer, you must respond to this change. The computer is becoming almost as commonplace as the TV in the home, and it needs somewhere to live. If you have the luxury of devoting a whole room to homeworking, and effectively creating an office, then this will certainly be a hit with many buyers. This room is often the rear reception room in a Victorian terrace, especially if the kitchen has been extended or is big enough to be a kitchen/breakfast room and so can accommodate your living needs. Alternatively, you may have another small room in the property that could work well as an office. Remember that we're not just talking about a computer base and a screen here – the serious homeworker needs a workstation and a chair, with room for a printer, fax, phone, as well as additional shelving for files, reference books, etc. On a practical level you'll need to equip the room with enough electricity and phone sockets to enable your purchaser to get down to work as soon as they move in. If you don't have an actual room to spare to serve as a study you can always create a pullout office in a secondary bedroom, with folding wardrobe doors to hide away all your clutter.

The great outdoors

The garden is another room of the house and must be treated as such. It may be a room that is rarely used but that's not the point. You must be able to see it from inside the property and know that there is the option to use it. The faint possibility of spending long, balmy evenings sipping white wine on the patio is what you are offering.

The idea of a garden

Britain, as we know, does not always have the hot sunny climate we all wish it did. The garden, therefore, plays a rather unusual role in our lives. It is something that we wish for, but, if we're honest, the majority of us would admit that we don't actually want the hassle of it. When developing property remember that your outside space is NEVER too small to bother about. If you only have a roof terrace (see page 116) you should still think of it as a valuable space. Plan carefully and use your imagination.

Southwest-facing gardens are generally considered the most desirable as they tend to get the afternoon sun – however, in urban areas, this will be affected by the length of your garden and also by what overlooks it. The easiest way to judge is to go into the garden at different times of the day and see where the sun falls. Don't forget that the sun is higher in the summer than in winter so where it falls may vary according to the seasons. Think about when your property is going on the market and ensure that at that time of year the garden will be looking at its absolute best.

Beat the competition

To call Britain's weather unreliable would be an understatement, so your aim is to be able to view and enjoy the garden from the property without having to actually go into it. Fit a large window or ideally glazed doors to look over the garden, with a sight line that allows you to appreciate your outside space from inside.

Who is your garden for?

If families are your main target market you'll need to lay some lawn for the children to play on. A busy professional will want to be able to enjoy the garden at the weekends and on summer evenings, but will not want to spend much time on maintenance, so avoid a lawn that will need mowing; and if the property is on the ground floor, bed plants into the earth rather than into pots that will need watering.

⊃ Practical tips for saleable gardens

- Start planning your outside space at the same time as you plan your inside space. If you can, use what you already have and improve it. The following tips will help you save time and money.

- Overgrown lawns that look like a meadow can be cut back down but make sure you leave enough time to cut them right down *and* for the regrowth to come through.

- Hedges and bushes that have taken over the garden need a thorough cut-back, and must be regularly trimmed during the running of a site.

- Keep any bricks that you pull out of the property – they may be useful for paving.

- Provide added privacy by ensuring that fences are of a reasonable height. Your neighbours may be willing to contribute to the cost of fencing but if they are not, do it anyway.

- Treat the garden as a daytime room (see page 78) and ensure you enter it from another day room – to have it leading off a bedroom is better than having no garden at all, but will always narrow your range of potential purchasers.

⊃ Landscape gardeners

If you are developing a top-end property, are pressed for time or are feeling entirely lost as to where to start with your garden, I'd advise you to call in the experts. It's fine to give a landscape gardener a completely blank slate and see what they come up with. Alternatively, if you've a clearer idea of what you're after, provide a drawing. Some landscape gardeners will give you advice that you can pay for on an hourly basis and then you can do the work yourself, but always ask them to quote to actually do the work as well, as they are able to buy plants and materials at a reduced price. The savings you make here, plus the time that is freed up for you to get on with other tasks, tends to mean that employing a landscape gardener doesn't actually cost that much, relatively speaking. The result, and the effect it has on your resale price, is very much worth the added expense.

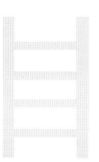

Your outside space is
NEVER too small to
bother about

⊃ The roof terrace

If there is any way you can have a roof terrace in a flat that is on the first floor or higher, this precious outside space will add thousands to the value of the property. You'll need planning permission for a terrace if one does not already exist. Look out of all windows and see if there is either an existing flat roofed area or an area that is pitched that could be made flat. Roof terraces are features on top of another piece of building, so if you get permission you are more likely to be allowed to create the terrace if you have a two-storey flat and own the part of the building that the roof terrace will sit on. Bear in mind that it is quite difficult to get this permission, as having a roof terrace means you're likely to overlook your neighbours' property and (fortunately) planning departments are very keen to protect people's privacy. If you do get permission you will need to comply with building regulations to ensure it is suitable to be walked on.

Kerb appeal

Equally important as the back garden is the front garden. After all, this is the very first thing your potential buyer will see! Front gardens are often overlooked but even if your front garden is tiny, it's worth spending time and effort making it look neat, tidy and welcoming. Keep lawns well trimmed and the area clear of rubbish. Avoid frightening your buyers before they even reach the front door with highly personal garden items such as sculptures, extravagant water features or any other item that reflects your personal taste.

To achieve kerb appeal you must focus on the exterior of the property as well as the front garden. It's amazing what a fresh coat of paint can do to the appearance of your home. If the window ledges need painting, do it; same for the front door and the gate. If the doorbell doesn't work, fix it, and if the windows need cleaning, get out the chamois. Your aim is to get the buyer in a positive frame of mind to view the rest of the property.

⊃ Communal gardens

Many flats have communal gardens, the upkeep of which is the joint responsibility of all the tenants/owners. If you have invested in such a property and this space is in a mess, then take the initiative and sort it out – you're the one who'll suffer if you don't. You will need to discuss any improvements or changes you want to make with the freeholder or managing agent. All flats in the building should contribute towards the work. Check the terms of your lease and ask the landlord or managing agents if they have objections. If they are happy for you to do the work, tell your neighbours what you're up to and just get on with it – mow the lawn, do some weeding and have a thorough tidy. After all, who's going to object to getting a nicer garden?

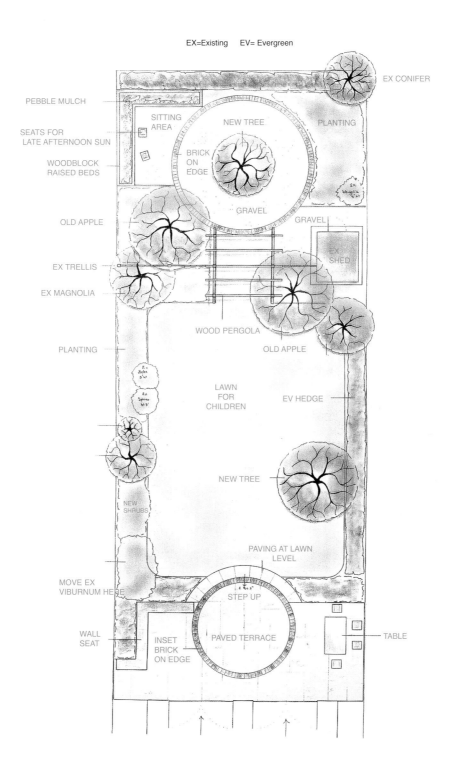

EX=Existing   EV= Evergreen

EX CONIFER

PEBBLE MULCH

SITTING
AREA

NEW TREE

PLANTING

SEATS FOR
LATE AFTERNOON SUN

BRICK
ON
EDGE

WOODBLOCK
RAISED BEDS

GRAVEL

OLD APPLE

GRAVEL

EX
SHED

EX TRELLIS

EX MAGNOLIA

WOOD PERGOLA

PLANTING

OLD APPLE

LAWN
FOR
CHILDREN

EV HEDGE

NEW TREE

NEW
SHRUBS

PAVING AT LAWN
LEVEL

MOVE EX
VIBURNUM HERE

STEP UP

WALL
SEAT

INSET
BRICK
ON EDGE

PAVED TERRACE

TABLE

Sorting out the final jobs

Whether you have done all or none of the work yourself, at the end of the renovation and refurbishment you need to compile a snagging list of those little jobs that you just didn't get round to when you were working on the individual rooms. If you neglect these jobs you could be putting your profit in jeopardy.

Walk round the finished property with a pad of paper and write down all the little jobs that still need to be done – removing that bit of paint from the light switch surround, fitting a missing screw in a door handle, painting a doorstep that has been missed. Once you have compiled your snagging list (see example, opposite), collect the tools you need to do all the jobs and get on with it. Individually these jobs are quick and easy, but getting the whole lot done may well take longer than you think.

There is no real harm in leaving something for the buyer to do. Don't worry if you cannot afford to do everything possible to a property you are developing – overdevelopment, when you have pushed the building out in every direction and maximised and utilised every inch of space, can make the property feel as if it is bursting at the seams. Leaving a self-contained job for the buyers that won't disrupt their day-to-day living too much will help them visualise themselves in the property and give them the enthusiasm to get going. Roof extensions are a perfect example – if you are selling a three-bedroomed house and your purchaser is uncertain whether they need three or four bedrooms, they can buy your property for less than they would pay for a four-bedroomed property and spend the money on creating the fourth bedroom when they need it, instead of having to move again.

Overdevelopment can make the property feel as if it is bursting at the seams

Checklist – snagging

GENERAL

Make sure all light bulbs work ☐

GARDEN (FRONT AND BACK)

Clear rubble sacks ☐

Clean windows ☐

Cut hedge ☐

HALLWAY

Screw back light switch ☐

Touch up paintwork inside
front door ☐

Fit letterbox ☐

LIVING ROOM

Paint hearth black ☐

Remove paint from light switch ☐

Touch up ceiling around
pendant ☐

KITCHEN

Silicone worktop ☐

Connect oven ☐

Clean sink ☐

BEDROOM

Fit hanging rail and handles
to wardrobes ☐

Remove paint from radiator ☐

Touch up paint on skirting ☐

BATHROOM

Bleach loo ☐

Fit plug on basin ☐

Clean paint off tiles ☐

Targeting the right market

Previous owners of Stuart's house had removed the original Victorian bay window and replaced it with an inappropriate square bay with glazed porch. His budget would not stretch to reinstating the original.

London-based actor Stuart Bowman wanted to get his foot on the property ladder so that he could eventually buy a property in trendy Notting Hill. He had a very limited budget so planned to do all the work himself.

The Budget £

Property bought for	£90,500
Projected cost of works	£3,000
Projected sale price	£110,000
Projected gross profit	£16,500 (17.6%)

What he bought

With a hefty mortgage, Stuart bought a two-bed terraced house in Plaistow, east London. The ground floor had a knocked-through living/dining room that was partly separated by an open staircase running through the middle of the room. The living room led to a kitchen and beyond that was a small junk room. Upstairs were two double bedrooms and one bathroom.

Plaistow did not show any obvious signs of being an up-and-coming area. It had a reputation for being a bit rough – Stuart admitted that he would have been reluctant to let his girlfriend walk home alone late at night – and had only basic grocery stores and cheap discount shops for household goods. On the plus side it was fairly near the City of London and this suggested property prices would eventually come up. However, that is speculation, and after all, with property development it is the work you do rather than what the market does that makes your money.

The plan

Stuart had straightforward ideas of how to increase the value of his property. He wanted to strip the floors in the living room, remove the old 1960s gas fire and have a modern fireplace behind it, and fit banisters to the staircase. He also wanted to fit a new kitchen, turn the junk room into an office, carpet the bedrooms upstairs and buy a new bathroom suite. He planned to wave goodbye to the outdated decoration and in the garden have a general tidy-up and lay a new lawn.

When the carpet was removed from the living room to reveal the original floorboards, Stuart unexpectedly discovered a lump of concrete. Buying antique floorboards to replace this area would have been expensive so, with the help of his ex-builder friend, Richie, Stuart decided to use some boards from the bedroom. These were the same age and colour as those on the ground floor so made a perfect match. He bought new floorboards to replace the ones in the bedroom but the style of these was not important as he carpeted the bedrooms anyway. He hired a floor sander for two days and sanded the floorboards in the downstairs rooms himself. It was a dirty job and physically demanding but was the cheapest way to achieve the floors he wanted.

For the kitchen, Stuart unfortunately succumbed to the lure of the free kitchen design service offered by a kitchen showroom. This led him to splash out on a brand new

Stuart was on a limited budget and needed to use as much of what already existed in the house as possible. A lot of elbow grease and some strong bleach turned a tired and dirty-looking bathroom into a bright, clean space.

Any property will appeal more to buyers when the flowers are in full bloom and the sun is shining. If you can arrange your viewings to take advantage of the times when your garden is looking at its best, then do so.

stainless-steel kitchen. He also removed the linoleum flooring and replaced it with slate tiles (which he used for the office as well).

He paid his friend Magic to build a banister (just one, even though Magic had advised him that one *either* side of the staircase would have been better), and in the bathroom replaced the loo seat, ripped up the carpet and put wood veneer flooring down, and gave it a thorough clean. Stuart was fortunate to find a sink in a skip that was a perfect fit, so he saved himself some money on the bathroom. Finally, he carpeted the stairs, bedrooms and upstairs hallway with seagrass and painted most of the house off-white.

The ceiling price

This is the highest price you can get for your property (see page 42). By looking at similar properties in Plaistow we discovered that the ceiling price for Stuart's house was unlikely to be more than £115,000. There would be only one way to break that ceiling, and that would be to add a room. The most common way of doing this is via a loft conversion (see pages 79 to 81), but a proper conversion can be very expensive. Stuart did have the space to build a third bedroom in the loft, but would it be worth more than it cost? He investigated the price of three-bedroomed houses in Plaistow and realised that the ceiling price was around £120,000. So, the extra room would increase his ceiling price by £5,000 but would cost him at least £10,000 to create. So it was back to the original plan – to make the most of the space he had! If Stuart had failed to investigate the ceiling price of three-bedroomed houses he might have gone ahead with the conversion, thereby throwing more money down the drain.

My advice

CREATE A GOOD FINISH. Stuart blew his budget on a new kitchen and trendy carpets instead of focusing on a good finish. There's no point spending £2,000 on a new kitchen if you're going to do a botched job on the tiling. I advised Stuart to paint the living room a warmer, slightly darker hue to give it a cottagey feel that would be more forgiving of the lumps and bumps on his less-than-perfect walls. That contemporary look is great, but only if you've got really flat surfaces to work with.

AVOID WASTEFUL SPENDING. It's not the size of your budget, it's what you do with it that counts, especially when you're on the bottom rung of the property ladder! I therefore advised Stuart to forget the new kitchen and make the most of the existing one by keeping the lino, which was in good condition, and buying a new worktop, splashback, tiles and new unit doors. I thought he should use the small junk room to create a breakfast/dining room rather than an office, by removing the adjoining door so that the new eating area would lead naturally from the kitchen. I advised Stuart to paint the kitchen a fairly dark colour to make it more warm and inviting and to prevent it from feeling like an annex to the kitchen. Finally, I thought he should buy end-of-line carpet or find a cheap carpet warehouse. Stuart did go to a cheap outlet, but he forked out £1,200 for trendy seagrass. Cheaper carpet would have cost him a quarter of that figure.

CONSIDER SPACE AND LAYOUT. He could have broadened his market by making the knocked-through living room into two separate rooms. Stuart was marketing his house to a young family and this market enjoys the flexibility of being able to close off one of the living areas. All he needed to do was build a stud wall by the staircase, which would have cost as little as £400.

Stuart created the contemporary interior that HE dreamed of rather than thinking carefully about what sort of look would really appeal to the market he would be selling to.

Final sums

Property bought for	£90,500
Final cost of works including fees	**£7,000**
Target selling price	£110,000–£115,000
Target gross profit	**£12,500–£17,500 (12.8%–17.9%)**

Three estate agents visited the property and valued it as follows:

Agent 1 £115,000

'When you look closely it is very much a DIY job. It wouldn't have cost a lot more to finish the kitchen really well. Upstairs is plain, simple, neat and tidy.'

Agent 2 £115,000

'The living areas are excellent, well designed. I liked the colours, but he should have put in a second banister. The kitchen is too trendy, too modern. It should have been toned down to appeal to no specific taste.'

Agent 3 £110,000

'One banister is a bad idea, just think of the safety of young children. The room off the kitchen would have been more useful if it had been made into a breakfast room. The most likely buyer is a family so he should have gone for a more homely and traditional style.'

Stuart should have been marketing his property towards a young family. Having just one banister was a mistake.

There is no value in spending lots of money on a new kitchen if you're not going to fit it properly. Having a poor finish can cost you thousands, as buyers will be reluctant to pay a top price for a less-than-perfect property.

So according to two of the agents, Stuart stood to make a profit of £17,500.

The six months spent on the project were very stressful for Stuart and left him exhausted. Once the house was finished, he decided to live there himself for a few months then reassess whether to put it on the market. In terms of property development, this was a mistake. He needed to sell up and move on quickly. When you start out as a property developer you'll find that the first few projects are the hardest, as you have less experience, less knowledge, more limited funds and therefore a more limited budget. But rest assured – it does get easier if you stick with it. You need to turn over as many properties as possible as quickly as possible to climb up the property ladder. **(2001)**

Where are they now?

Stuart sat on his property for another year and, mainly due to the market rising, eventually sold it for £150,000, making him a fantastic £52,500 profit! Stuart is currently staying with his girlfriend in Notting Hill, west London, and looking to invest his profit in a flat in Glasgow, which he intends to renovate and rent out to give him a comforting income. **(2002)**

6
THE
SALE

OK, so it's the moment you've been waiting for. The moment when you see whether all your research, your careful budgeting and the improvements you have made are going to pay off. But before you get to the complexities of agents, solicitors, viewings and valuations, you must present your property for sale.

Presenting your property

How you present your finished product is the logical conclusion to all your refurbishment and design work. If you overlook this, for the buyer the experience of viewing will be the same as if they were to go to a nice restaurant, with beautiful food but slopped onto a dirty plate.

Clean, clean, clean

Cleaning is the first rule of presenting your property. It may sound obvious but when I say cleaning I really mean cleaning. There are companies that will carry out a 'builder's clean', which in theory sounds pretty thorough, but I have to say that virtually all the cleaning companies I have used have been disappointing – I still end up with my rubber gloves on! If in doubt, do it yourself. Other people's standards may simply not be high enough. And you'll save money.

You need to set aside at least a day for cleaning. A good approach is to create another 'snagging' list (as you did for unfinished decorating jobs – see page 119). This one should cover all the bases.

• Ensure the windows are spotless, both inside and out.

• Bathrooms must be clean and all taps sparkling (Viakal is great for this).

• Vacuum throughout to catch all those little bits of carpet left by the carpet fitters.

• Dust all the skirting.

• Check there is no paint on the light switches or sockets, doors or window furniture (handles, hinges, catches and locks).

• Check that all light bulbs work.

• Clean inside all cupboards and cabinets. Many buyers will find it impossible to resist the urge to open cupboard doors.

• Remove any piles of building rubbish from the garden.

• Go out onto the street. Look in both directions and ensure there are no obvious eyesores – an old pram, unwanted furniture, newspapers and crisp packets. If anything is spoiling the view of your property take it to the dump or put it in the bin.

Selling a lifestyle/styling

Presenting your property means offering an immaculately clean property. You can also carefully select pieces of furniture to suggest to potential purchasers how it might look if they were to live there. This is almost always done with larger multi-unit developments, in the form of the 'show home'. What you are doing is very similar. Large developers will either have an in-house specialist who creates the show home or will employ a company that designs the look, supplies the furniture and arranges it.

Of course you too can hire a showroom specialist, but it's another slice of your budget gone and you can almost certainly achieve the same result by taking carefully selected items from your own home and borrowing from accommodating relatives and friends.

Your aim is to create a space that invites people to come in, kick their shoes off, pour a large glass of wine and make themselves at home. However, if you're not confident that you can present the property in the right way, or are unable to get the right furniture without forking out considerable amounts of cash, leave it empty. Many properties look at their best with a beautiful finish, immaculately clean and with that great sense of space that an empty property gives.

Getting the presentation right is quite a delicate operation. The key is not to put too much in. You are not *furnishing* the property, you are *suggesting* how it could be lived in. Avoid the temptation to scatter favourite items and accessories around because you think this will give the property a welcoming a feel. It will be welcoming to you, but not necessarily to a broad market. These guidelines will help you crack the secrets of presentation.

KITCHEN

Keep the kitchen empty of utensils and kitchenware but add elements such as a bowl of fresh fruit, vase of flowers and/or some olive oil by the cooker. If you are presenting a kitchen/breakfast room put in the largest-sized table you can and the maximum number of chairs that fit comfortably around it without the room looking out of proportion.

LIVING AREAS

The dining room will look fine with just a table and perhaps a mirror on the mantelpiece to give the room more depth. In the sitting room avoid putting in an oversized sofa as it will feel awkward. A mirror is again a good idea. Put in enough pieces of furniture, perhaps an armchair or two or a coffee table, to make it feel comfortable but keep it simple and don't clutter the room.

You are not furnishing the property, you are *suggesting* how it could be lived in

BEDROOMS

The only essential piece of furniture is the bed. Buy any old bed from a second hand shop and dress is with a valance and crisp fresh linen. No one will ever sleep in the bed so this is an area where you can go for the cheapest possible and save money. But remember, keep the bed in proportion to the rest of the room. Avoid a choice of black and red satin sheets (unless that fits in with what you are trying to create!) as, believe it or not, some people won't like them.

ACCESSORIES

Mirrors are a great way of emphasising the size of a room and you can often prop them on a mantelpiece to avoid damaging the walls. If you have a large blank wall it is a good idea to create a focal point with a painting, the style of which complements the type of property, but avoid bashing holes all over the place with picture hooks. The new purchaser is buying your property because they DON'T want to redecorate.

FLOWERS

Highly scented flowers look great and give the property a wonderful perfume. Check them regularly and change the water. They must look as though they've just burst into flower. A vase of wilting, rotting flowers is a truly depressing (not to mention smelly) prospect.

Living in your product

If you're living in your property while trying to sell it you must accept that your priority is the presentation of the property for the buyer, not your personal comfort or day-to-day convenience. This may mean building extra time into your day to keep on top of things. You can't afford to go to work with piles of congealing plates in the sink because you couldn't face them the night before – you're paying your agent to sell your property and the agent can't always give 24 hours' notice of a viewing. The day you've left your underwear on the floor may be the one day that a genuinely interested buyer comes to view. Make a living-in checklist, either on paper or in your head:

Checklist – living in

Clear up clutter ☐

Don't leave dirty clothes about ☐

Don't leave clothes drying on airers or radiators ☐

Do all the washing-up AND putting away ☐

Avoid strong smells of dog, cat, cigarettes, spicy meals, etc. ☐

Keep carpets vacuumed ☐

Keep floors washed and swept ☐

Make all the beds every morning (and do it properly!) ☐

Keep the bathroom spotless ☐

Keep bathroom products in a cabinet ☐

Make sure bin bags are taken outside ☐

Don't leave personal papers and files lying around ☐

Don't leave the ironing board out ☐

Mow lawns, cut hedges and weed the garden regularly ☐

The best time to sell your property is as soon as it is finished. Having said that, there are annual cyclical movements in property, which are independent of long-term market movements. The extent to which you will be affected by these movements depends largely on whom you are marketing the property towards. If you are selling a large family house, children are on holiday in August and so families are less likely to be around. If they are around, dragging children around to view properties is unlikely to be high on any parent's agenda. Your property may look more appealing at a certain time of day but you will have to be led by the buyer's timetable requirements in this respect. Seriously interested buyers may wish to view the property at different times of the day to see how the light coming into the property varies. Once you have decided to put your property on the market your next job is to find a good solicitor and estate agent.

Solicitors and estate agents

There is no doubt in my mind that a good solicitor is the backbone of running any company, especially one that deals with property. You need a solicitor who not only knows and understands property law but who also has a great deal of experience and interest in it. Similarly, choosing the right estate agent to sell your property is essential. Much like builders, agents tend to get bad press. Much of this is undeserved and many agents are very knowledgeable, charming, helpful and, most important, good at their job.

Finding a solicitor

We've always used the same firm of solicitors and they have, over the years, not only saved us money with their knowledge and support but have also been an amazing anchor in an industry that is always volatile. Without them I'm sure we would not be where we are today. Luck played a part in finding our solicitor, but when you do find a good firm it is important to stick with it. It doesn't matter if your solicitor is based in a different town or city. Go for the best, not necessarily the closest. Don't be put off if a solicitor seems expensive. As a friend of mine always says, if you pay peanuts, you'll get monkeys. This is especially true with all aspects of property development.

Finding an estate agent

I believe you cannot SELL someone a house or flat, and by that I mean you cannot persuade someone to exchange on a property that is not exactly right for them. The sums involved are far too high. You might be able to persuade someone to offer on a property they are not that keen on but they are extremely unlikely to actually exchange. This wastes everybody's time, effort and money. If you agree with this logic then it follows that what an agent has to do is introduce the right purchaser to the right property. A good agent will be first and foremost a listener. By listening to the purchaser they will get a good idea of what will and will not be acceptable and then it's just a question of not putting them off. This comes down to basic people skills and a good dose of handholding throughout the process.

When choosing your agent, therefore, you must actually like them. If the agent listens and appears to understand your aims you're off to a great start. The agency should be one that is representing properties that are similar to yours, for an amount of money similar to your target sale price. Make sure you're completely happy with the level and standard of information provided on the details and that the agency talks you through where and how they plan to market it. In an ideal world you should try to sell your property through the estate agent who sold it to you. They can see what you've created from the original product and when the next suitable property comes up for sale they will hopefully be on the phone to you. Building long-term relationships with agents, solicitors, contractors and other working partners will give stability to your growing business and may spare you the disruption and lost time caused by endless changes.

In an ideal world you should try to sell your property through the estate agent who sold it to you

➥ The estate agent's valuation

I would suggest you get at least three or four agents to value your property. Do not necessarily go for the agent who has given it the highest valuation – it's much easier to get an agent to *say* a buyer will pay £x for your property than to find someone who actually will. Go with the agent who gives the valuation that you consider to be the most realistic, based on your research of similar properties in the area. It is much better to get three buyers who are genuinely interested in your property, and let them drive the price up between them, than to have no-one even prepared to look round. At the end of the day, as long as you expose it to the right market, all property will find its own value – that is the amount someone is prepared to pay for it.

Get ahead	Read the estate agency's small print very carefully to check that you are not tied into an agreement with them for months. Some will require written notice if you want to either instruct another agency at the same time or remove the property from their books.

➥ Working with your estate agent

As a general rule, I'd say don't waste time quibbling over agents' rates (unless you happen to be selling several dozen properties at a time). They will be working very hard to sell your property and arguing over a fraction of a percent will hardly leave you better off and could sour the relationship, meaning the agent might not put maximum effort into the sale. Having them work harder for you will pay off.

Put the property on a particular agent's books for a limited period only. When the agency first gets the property they will contact all the registered buyers they know might be interested and show them round. If three or four weeks go by without any firm interest the agency is basically waiting for the right person to come to *them* (while hopefully advertising to get further interest). The right person might walk through the door that afternoon but it's a bit hit and miss. You're better off changing agency and beginning the exercise again with that agency's registered applicants.

Types of agent

SOLE AGENT – this mean that you have instructed only one agent to work for you. The advantage of this type of arrangement is that as soon as the agent gets an offer they will know that the property is no longer being viewed. The contract you sign with a sole agent will commit you to not offering the property to any other agency for a specific period.

JOINT SOLE AGENTS – this is when you instruct two agencies in order to achieve wider coverage. With this type of arrangement the agencies have an agreement whereby the one that sells the property takes the majority of your fee and the other a smaller percentage.

MULTIPLE AGENTS – this will expose your property to more of the market, but is not always the best option. If a potential buyer (who, let's face it, is likely to have signed up with several if not all the agents in the area) is getting details of your property from half a dozen different agencies this may give the impression you are desperate to sell and therefore bring the price down. It can also confuse the buyer if property descriptions and prices differ. A maximum of three agencies is a good compromise.

Selling privately – a word of warning

On paper, a private sale sounds like a great money saver. Wouldn't it be great not to have to pay those agents' fees! In reality, it means a huge amount of organisation – arranging and carrying out all the viewings yourself, being responsible for the marketing of the property – and no intermediary if things go wrong. And you still have to pay the solicitor's fees. Personally I'd always advise selling your property through an agent. They are in the business of selling houses and flats, and are familiar with every aspect of the process – the marketing, viewings and negotiating. Negotiating the sale of a property is not nearly as easy as it sounds. There is a great deal of money on the line and tensions can run high. Having someone to act as the link between you and your purchaser can alleviate no end of problems. What's more, an agent is in the best position to justify your asking price with comparable sales to any potential purchaser. The purchaser will know that the agent has their finger on the pulse – after all, this is what they do day in day out – and will know that your asking price is in line with what other properties have recently been on sale for.

Letting agents

So far we have considered agents, valuations and viewings from the point of view of the developer who is selling properties. If you are letting your property to tenants, however, different rules and priorities apply, though there are some common denominators.

Using an agent or going it alone?

If you are renting out your property your first decision is whether you are going to use a letting agent or do the whole thing yourself. If you decide to use an agent you then have the option of using the agent to market the property and introduce a potential tenant only, or to manage the let throughout the term of the tenancy as well.

If it is your first property I would recommend that you at least use an agent to find your tenant (see 'Introduction Service', over). However, if you are determined to take charge of the letting process yourself this section will tell you what to look out for. Letting yourself can save you 15% of your income that you would be paying to an agent.

What does a letting agent do?

Most letting agents offer you a choice in the type of service they provide, which can basically be split into the following:

FULL MANAGEMENT SERVICE

This is when the agent advertises your property, finds a tenant, checks references, compiles an inventory (see Appendix 2, pages 153 to 154), moves the tenants in, and throughout the tenancy collects the rent and deals with any problems that may arise during the lifespan of the agreement (including arranging for contractors if needed, the cost of which will be deducted from your monthly rental payments). This type of arrangement is ideal if you are either very busy, have no idea how to deal with the general maintenance of the property or live a long way away, perhaps even abroad. For the Full Management Service an agency will generally charge about 15% of your rental income.

INTRODUCTION AND RENT COLLECTION

This is the same service except that when problems arise instead of the agency sending in their contractors and deducting the cost from your rent they will phone you and you can either deal with it yourself or send your own contractors in to sort out the problem. You will be charged about 12.5% of your rental income for this service, and you may be able to make savings on the actual work by doing it or arranging it yourself.

INTRODUCTION SERVICE

This is when the letting agency's role is limited to marketing the property and finding a tenant. When the tenant moves in all responsibilities revert to you. You must therefore create the inventory, check the rent is paid on time and deal with the situation if it is not. You are also the direct point of contact should problems arise with the property. For the introduction service you are likely to be charged about 10% of your rental income.

Furnishing a rental property

Whichever letting option you go for, you will need to decide whether to offer the property furnished or unfurnished. Think about your target market and whether prospective tenants are likely to want to bring their own furniture with them. Young home leavers will probably just have a suitcase, so provide them with curtains, carpets, sofas, beds, wardrobes and a table and chairs, though don't forget that the more items you provide the more potential damage there is. The kitchen is a key area. I would advise that you provide only the white goods (a fridge, washing machine and cooker) and let the tenants buy the rest. The exception is letting to students, who will expect a kitchen fully stocked with basic cutlery, plates, bowls, mugs, pots and pans, etc (see the inventory in Appendix 2, pages 153 to 154). Similarly, short-term, high-end rentals generally expect everything they need to be there on tap as they are paying a premium for this convenience (see Case Study, pages 138 to 143).

The lists opposite are GUIDES ONLY. The terms 'fully furnished' and 'unfurnished' do tend to mean different things with different agents and different markets, so your best bet is to take advice from a local lettings agent. At the end of the day, it's down to you.

The following general rules also apply:

• All tenants would prefer the furniture, especially the beds, to be new. Therefore don't worry too much about investing in furniture that will last a long time. It's better to buy a new bed each time the tenancy changes hands than to spend five times as much and replace it every five years.

• Use a limited number of paint colours in a rental property and make sure you keep a note of the colour code and make of the paint in a safe place. This way, if you need to repaint a wall during a tenancy changeover you'll not only be able to lay your hands on the right colour quickly but you'll also avoid having to lug fifteen different paint pots around (and pay for them).

• Go for manmade carpets rather than woollen ones – our carpet cleaner (who can make even the most disgusting carpets look brand new) swears that manmade carpets are easier to clean than woollen. Choose a darker shade of carpet than you normally would so marks are less likely to show.

• Ensure all your furniture complies with the Furniture and Furnishings (Fire) (Safety) Regulations 1988.

Checklist – furnishing rental properties

UNFURNISHED

Nothing except a cooker ☐

PART-FURNISHED

Washing machine ☐

Fridge-freezer ☐

Cooker ☐

Dishwasher [optional] ☐

Wardrobes ☐

Chest of drawers (optional) ☐

Beds ☐

Sofa ☐

Curtains and blinds ☐

FULLY-FURNISHED (OR FURNISHED)

Washing machine ☐

Fridge-freezer ☐

Cooker ☐

Dishwasher [optional] ☐

Wardrobes ☐

Chest of drawers ☐

Beds ☐

Sofa ☐

Curtains and blinds ☐

Lamp shades ☐

Coffee table ☐

Table and chairs (if space) ☐

SHORT-TERM LET (CORPORATE LET)

Washing machine ☐

Fridge-freezer ☐

Cooker ☐

Dishwasher [optional] ☐

Wardrobes ☐

Chest of drawers ☐

Beds ☐

Sofa ☐

Curtains and blinds ☐

Lamp shades ☐

Coffee table ☐

Table and chairs ☐

Crockery ☐

Glasses ☐

Cutlery ☐

Toaster ☐

Kettle ☐

A full set of linens on the beds ☐

Towels ☐

All soft furnishings ☐

TV ☐

Video ☐

Hi-fi ☐

DVD [optional] ☐

Marketing a short-term let

Melanie's flat had its own front door – always a plus for any potential buyer.

Melanie Bradley is a freelance researcher in her early thirties living in London. After developing a three-bedroomed house, that she lived in and sold for a £60,000 profit, Melanie caught the property bug in a big way.

The Budget

£

Melanie used the profit that she made on the sale of her previous home to pay for the development of her new investment.

Property bought for	£169,000
Projected cost of works	£40,000
Mortgage repayments	£370 per week
Projected rental price	£700 per week
Projected gross profit	£330 per week

Creating a loft extension is a great way to add an extra room. Just make sure you get all your permissions in place before you start the work.

What she bought

Melanie decided to target the expanding corporate rental market based in and around Chiswick, in southwest London, and to develop a high-quality apartment for short-term letting.

The property she found had one bedroom and two box rooms. She felt the property was ripe for development.

It was important for Melanie to choose her area very carefully. The location had to have both the right market and enough major businesses and employment opportunities to justify the high rent. Chiswick, eight miles from Heathrow and only five miles from the centre of London, yet quiet and leafy and with many trendy shops, restaurants and boutiques, was the perfect choice. It also had a large business park under development nearby, which would provide an estimated 10,000 office jobs. Melanie had bought very wisely indeed.

The plan

Melanie decided to convert the property into a luxury two-bed apartment by putting in a loft conversion. The flat had a good-sized kitchen and a small bathroom so she planned to enlarge the kitchen by ripping out the existing bathroom and knocking through the dividing wall. One of the box rooms would then become a study while the other would make way for the stairs into the loft conversion, where the new main bedroom and bathroom would be located. Melanie also planned to use the wide hallway to create a small walk-in shower room, which would be accessed via the hallway.

When providing items of crockery and cutlery for rental properties always use stylish, matching pieces but make sure they are easily replaceable.

My advice

I thought Melanie should break down her £40,000 budget as follows:

Loft conversion	£20,000
Bathrooms	£5,000
Kitchen	£7,000
Building and decorating	£8,000
Total	£40,000

By removing the bathroom at the back of the property, Melanie opened up the room and created enough space for a table and chairs – a real plus for any potential renters.

I also advised her to:

MAKE THE MOST OF OUTSIDE SPACE. Any outside space can add value to a property – especially an urban one. Mel had steps leading down to a garden at the back of the flat so I advised her to build a little veranda to maximise the garden's potential.

ORGANISE INTERNAL LAYOUT ACCORDING TO THE MARKET. I advised Mel to rethink the use of the existing kitchen and bathroom space. I agreed with her that she should knock down the wall separating the kitchen and the bathroom, but I thought she should take some space at the *back* of the kitchen and create a full bathroom there, so that the kitchen could overlook the garden. I also thought that, given she could have created an extra bathroom in the kitchen, the hallway space would be best used as a walk-in wardrobe accessed via the bedroom rather than a walk-in shower room accessed via the hallway.

Furnishing a short-term let

It's important not to scrimp and save when furnishing a flat for this kind of high-end rental market. A corporate client is going to expect very high standards and, as they are only there for a short period, you need to offer them a fully equipped, ready-to-live-in property. Buy new but have loose covers on the sofa so that they can be washed between tenancies. Keep a spare set as well so that the turnaround between tenants can be sped up. Think durable and neutral. Buy crockery and cutlery which is plain and not from a sale – discontinued and patterned plates and glasses will be impossible to replace in the likely event of any breakage. Decorate in light colours as they are smart and upmarket but do not overfill the house with furniture and accessories. A good-sized bathroom with a powerful shower is a must as are a complete supply of linens and a properly equipped kitchen. Ideally supply a TV with cable/satellite, a hi-fi and a DVD player.

This project involved a lot of building work and complete modernisation. A loft conversion isn't cheap and in the long run may not add the amount it costs to build onto the value of the house. Your local council will tell you if you need planning permission but make sure you get it before you start work. With her very tight schedule (just eight weeks to complete the whole project), Melanie decided to start work without planning permission, which I would never recommend. By week eight, when the development was scheduled to have finished, she was still waiting to hear back from the planning office. Luckily, permission was eventually granted but the site had over-run by five weeks. In other words she had lost £3,500 in potential rent and had to cover an extra mortgage payment she had not bargained for – money down the drain!

Anyone renting a corporate flat will expect top-quality accessories like digital wide-screen TVs. Leaving out these little extras might lose you tenants and therefore profit.

Melanie was set on the idea of a large kitchen. Instead of catering for the fast-living, microwave-zapping corporate market, she was thinking of the kitchen *she* wanted. As a result, she invested in an expensive and luxurious kitchen, although she did follow the advice of a kitchen designer whose design worked out an astonishing £5,000 cheaper than her own. You *will* need to fit high-quality cupboards, surfaces and appliances in a corporate-let kitchen, but the cost can be minimised by keeping the kitchen small. A huge kitchen is unnecessary – it simply won't get a huge amount of use. Corporate workers tend to work late, eat out and probably only really want to use the microwave.

Developing rental property can be a lucrative long-term investment and the corporate market can bring particularly high rewards, though the risks are higher. If tenants not only require exceptional standards but also change frequently, you must have a reasonable amount of money available at all times to fit out the property with high-quality fixtures. The risk of the property lying empty for periods at a stretch can be high, but get it right and you'll command some of the highest rental prices around.

Final sums

Property bought for	£169,000
Final cost of works including fees:	
Loft	£20,000
Bathrooms	£8,000
Kitchen	£15,000
Building	£16,000
Fixtures and fittings	£6,000
Total	**£65,000**

Melanie got the following quotes from local lettings agents:

Agent 1	let for £695 per week
Agent 2	let for £725 per week
Agent 3	let for £750 per week

The site did over-run by five weeks and went £25,000 over budget. However, a major oversight was that in her original budget she had no money assigned to fixtures and fittings at all! In spite of this, the end product was a stunning, light and airy flat that looked certain to fetch the required £700 per week rental. What's more, it was valued at a remarkable £325,000, so if Melanie had decided to sell, she would have made a whopping £91,000 gross profit. **(2001)**

Melanie decided to utilise the space available in the hallway to provide an internal ensuite shower room with very contemporary fittings.

Where are they now?

Unfortunately when Melanie finished the work on the flat it was at a time when no corporate lets were really shifting. She therefore decided to change tack and live in the flat herself and to remortgage the property to obtain funds with which to continue her property development career. Since then she has renovated four properties in West London: two flats in Chiswick, which she has sold, and two in White City, which she is planning to rent out. **(2002)**

➲ Do-it-yourself letting

If you have decided to bypass the lettings agent and manage the property yourself here is a step-by-step guide to making it as smooth a ride as possible.

ADVERTISE

Place an ad in your local paper or in a specialist property publication and keep the description of the property simple and to the point, mentioning only the key features such as number of rooms and closeness to transport, as well as the monthly or weekly rental, and when the property is available. When people ring up be as realistic as possible in your description. There is no point in luring prospective tenants in under false pretences, you'll just spend more time organising viewings than you need to.

PLAN YOUR VIEWINGS

You will find that quite a high percentage of people who make appointments to view your property will not bother turning up – it's one of the hazards of the job. Accept it and arrange for everyone to view at the same time rather than at 15-minute intervals. This means you won't end up sitting around for hours.

DON'T DELAY

If someone does want to take the property, don't cancel other viewings until you have received a CASH deposit from them. I would advise against accepting a cheque as a deposit as there is always the chance it could bounce or be cancelled. Explain very clearly to the tenants that this is a non-refundable deposit and that if they change their minds and decide they don't want the property after all they will not get the deposit money refunded. Provide them with a written receipt for the deposit, take their details and give them yours, agreeing on a date for them to move in. Make it clear to them that the funds for the first month's rent and deposit must have cleared into YOUR account before they can move in. Ask them to forward you all the references you require – previous landlord, employer, bank and any other references you feel are necessary.

Get ahead	With rental properties you should try to ensure that your tenants do not use Blu-tac on the walls. This is because the oils in the Blu-tac will seep through further coats of emulsion (so repainting does not help).

PREPARE TWO COPIES OF THE TENANCY AGREEMENT

This is a document the tenants will send to their bank to enable a standing order to be set up for the monthly payment. Examples of assured shorthold tenancies, which are normally made out for 6 or 12 months, can be found in Appendix 1, pages 148 to 152. You need to give them your own bank details and enclose two copies of the inventory (see Appendix 2, pages 153 to 154). Before moving in both you and the tenants need to sign both copies of the tenancy agreement in the presence of an independent witness. Then keep one copy each.

PROVIDE SAFETY GUARANTEES

As landlord you must provide your tenants with a gas safety certificate if there is a gas supply to the property – these cost around £25 from a CORGI-registered plumber. You also need to ensure that you have appropriate smoke alarms fitted (battery-powered ones can be bought from Argos) and that your furnishings are fire-retardant if they are made after 1950. Meeting these requirements is the responsibility of the landlord and you are legally bound to abide by these rules.

GO THROUGH THE INVENTORY

On moving day meet the tenants to give them their keys (keeping the original, because if you need to make copies it's best to cut these from the original). Both you and the tenants need to check the inventory together and sign to show you agree it is accurate. Give the tenants a copy, together with a copy of the gas safety certificate.

AND THAT'S IT!... just sit back and wait for the money to come in. UNTIL… the boiler breaks down, the cooker won't work, the shower hose starts leaking, damp appears or the washing machine goes on the blink. Only then will you discover how you are really earning your money. But of course, you can do a great deal to minimise the chances of problems occurring by choosing your property carefully in the first place and being practical in your choice of materials and furniture. A tenant will inevitably take less care of a property than an owner will so you need to make the property more hardwearing, particularly the kitchen and bathroom. Here are some tips:

• If the silicone around the bath, shower, sink and kitchen worktop is cracked cut it out and re-silicone the affected area.

• Extractor fans in the kitchen and bathroom will help keep condensation away without opening a window and should help the rooms look good for longer.

• Ensure you have enough splashbacks in the bathrooms to stop the walls from getting damaged.

➲ Tenancy changeovers

When your tenants give notice that they want to vacate the property ensure they understand that in accordance with the terms of their tenancy agreement the property must be vacated in the same condition as it was occupied (except fair wear and tear). If your tenants do not leave the property in this condition you are entitled to retain some of their deposit to pay someone else to bring the property back up to scratch. Changeovers are a hassle. They involve lots of running around on your part to ensure the property is in tip-top condition when it's handed over to the new tenants. Therefore, it's best to pay a visit when your existing tenants first hand in their notice so that you can get a rough idea of the type and amount of work required and plan accordingly. Give plenty of notice of your visit – the tenancy agreement states that your tenants have a right to live in the property undisturbed until it is time for them to move out (see clause 2.10 on page150).

➲ Managing landlord-tenant relations

If rental properties are being run successfully then both you and your tenants should have an easy life. Most tenants don't want to hear from you any more than you want to hear from them. They just want to live in the property, avoid any hassle, pay their rent and get on with their lives. You just want to collect the rent every month, avoid any hassle and get on with your life. So remember – if something goes wrong in the property deal with it, and immediately if it is causing a major inconvenience. If the boiler breaks down in midwinter that can reasonably qualify as a major inconvenience. Get it sorted out, regardless of cost, within 24 hours. If you build up a good professional relationship with your tenants they are more likely to want to stay in your property, so sparing you the cost and time involved in changeovers. This is ultimately the position you want to be in with regard to your tenants.

TAKING IT FURTHER...

Well done! You have achieved a successful sale. Now you can work out how much actual profit you made and compare it against your original costings. If you have followed all my advice in this book your final sums should show that all the hard work was worth it and you will be one step closer to your own personal goal. Your next move is to think about whether you want to do it again. I hope you do.

If you are feeling flush with the success of your first project and eager to make this your full-time career and start developing at full speed, you will need to consult with your accountant on future tax planning. Your accountant will have advised you how to keep your accounts during the running of the site and will already be familiar with the nature of your fledgling business. The right route forward depends on what other sources of income you have and on what other commitments you have in your life. This is not the place to go into the tax implications of the various options on offer – that would be an entirely new book – but of course you need to be aware that you must pay tax on any profit you make. The good news is that to pay tax you have to have made a profit – so congratulations!

If, on the other hand, you have come to the conclusion that developing is not for you, I hope you have been able to take away some of the information and put it to good use anyway. The very fact that you have read this book means you share my fascination with property – so good luck with all your building ventures. Remember, it's not a crime to buy a house just because you want a home.

TENANCY AGREEMENT

(FOR A FURNISHED FLAT OR HOUSE ON AN ASSURED SHORTHOLD TENANCY)

THE PROPERTY

....

....

THE LANDLORD

....

    of ....

....

THE TENANT/S

....

....

The **TERM** ....   **months beginning on** ....

The **RENT** **£**..................... **per week/month***

      payable in advance on the............. **of each**......... **week/month***
                     (*Please delete as appropriate)

The **DEPOSIT £**........................

DATED this .... **day of** ....**200_.**

SIGNED

....
  (The LANDLORD)   **(The TENANT/S)**

THIS RENTAL AGREEMENT COMPRISES THE PARTICULARS DETAILED ABOVE, THE TERMS AND CONDITIONS ATTACHED AND THE INVENTORY SIGNED BY THE LANDLORD AND TENANT.

IMPORTANT NOTES FOR LANDLORDS

The "LANDLORD's" details on this Agreement must include an address for the Landlord in England or Wales as well as his/her name.
Written Notice to Terminate to the Tenant must be given two clear months before the end of the Term.

(THE FORM REFERRED TO ABOVE: – NOTICE TO TERMINATE IS AVAILABLE ON WWW.LETONTHENET.COM LANDLORDS ADVICE PAGE.)

Every effort has been taken to make this Agreement as easy to use as possible. There may be situations that make this form inappropriate for use, therefore if you are in any doubt as to your legal rights under this agreement then you should seek professional advice and assistance from a Solicitor, Housing Advice Centre or the CAB. Letonthenet.com cannot be held liable in respect of any loss or damage caused or alleged to be caused directly or indirectly by what is contained or omitted from this document.

Terms and Conditions

(FOR A FURNISHED FLAT OR HOUSE ON AN ASSURED SHORTHOLD TENANCY)

1. This Agreement is intended to create an assured shorthold tenancy as defined in the Housing Act 1988 and the provisions for the recovery of possession by the Landlord in that Act apply accordingly. The Tenant understands that the Landlord will be entitled to recover possession of the Property at the end of the Term

2. The Tenant will:

   2.1 pay the Rent at the times and in the manner aforesaid without any deduction abatement or set-off whatsoever (save for any deduction abatement or set-off allowable in law)

   2.2 pay all charges in respect of any electric, gas, water and telephonic or televisual services used at or supplied to the Property and Council Tax or any similar tax that might be charged in addition to or replacement of it during the Term

   2.3 keep the items on the inventory and the interior of the Property in a good, clean state and condition and not damage or injure the Property or the items on the Inventory

2.4 yield up the Property and the items on the Inventory at the end of the Term in the same clean state and condition it/they was/were in at the beginning of the Term (but the Tenant will not be responsible for fair wear and tear caused during normal use of the Property and the items on the Inventory or for any damage covered by and recoverable under the insurance policy effected by the Landlord under clause 3.2)

2.5 not make any alteration or addition to the property nor without the Landlord's prior written consent do any redecoration or painting of the Property

2.6 not do or omit to do anything on or at the Property which may be or become a nuisance or annoyance to the Landlord or owners or occupiers of adjoining or nearby premises, is illegal or immoral or which may in any way affect or prejudice the insurance of the Property and the items listed on the Inventory or cause an increase in the premium payable thereof

2.7 not without the Landlords prior consent allow or keep any pet or any kind of animal at the Property

2.8 not use or occupy the Property in any way whatsoever other than as a private residence

2.9 not assign, sublet, charge or part with or share possession occupation of the Property

2.10 permit the Landlord or anyone authorised by the Landlord at reasonable hours in the daytime and upon reasonable prior notice (except in emergency) to enter and view the Property for any proper purpose (including the checking of compliance with the Tenant's obligations under this Agreement and during the last month of the Term the showing of the Property to prospective new tenants)

2.11 pay interest at the rate of 4% above the Base Lending Rate for the time being of the Landlord's bankers upon any Rent or other money due from the Tenant under this agreement which is more than 3 days arrear in respect of the period from when it became due to the date of payment

3. The Landlord will:

3.1 subject to the Tenant paying the rent and performing his/her obligations under this agreement allow the Tenant peaceably to hold and enjoy the Property during the term without lawful interruption from Landlord or any person rightfully claiming under or in trust for the Landlord

3.2 insure the property and the items listed on the Inventory and use all reasonable efforts to arrange for any damage caused by an uninsured risk to be remedied without delay

3.3 keep in repair the structure and exterior of the property (including drains, gutters and external pipes)

3.4 keep in repair and proper working order the installations at the Property for the supply of water, gas and electricity and for sanitation (including basins, sinks, baths and sanitary conveniences)

3.5 keep in repair and proper working order the installation at the Property for space heating and heating water

But the Landlord will not be required to:

carry out works for which the tenant is responsible by virtue of his/her duty to use the property in a tenant-like manner

rebuild or reinstate the property in case of destruction or damage by fire or by tempest flood or other inevitable accident caused by or due to the Tenant failing to do and for which the insurers refuse to pay out or for which is not covered by the insurance policy effected by the Landlord

4. If at anytime

4.1 any part of the Rent is outstanding for 10 days after becoming due (whether formally demanded or not) and/or

4.2 there is any breach, non-observance or non-performance by the Tenant of any covenant or other term of this Agreement and/or

4.3 any interim receiver is appointed in respect of the Tenant's property or Bankruptcy Orders made in respect of the Tenant or the Tenant makes any arrangement with his creditors or suffers any distress or execution to be levied on his goods and/or

4.4 any of the grounds set out as Grounds 8 or Grounds 10–15 (inclusive) (which relate to breach of any obligation by a Tenant) contained in the Housing Act 1988 Schedule 2 apply

The Landlord may enter the property or any part of the property (and upon such re-entry this agreement shall absolutely determine but without prejudice to any claim which the Landlord may have against the Tenant in respect of any antecedent breach of any covenant or any term of this Agreement)

5. The Deposit has been paid by the Tenant and is held by the Landlord to secure compliance with the Tenant's obligations under this Agreement (without prejudice to the Landlords other rights and remedies) and if, at any time during the Term, the Landlord is obliged to draw upon it to satisfy any outstanding breaches of such obligations then the Tenant shall forthwith make such additional

payment as is necessary to restore the full amount of the Deposit held by the Landlord. As soon as reasonably practicable following termination of this Agreement the Landlord shall return to the Tenant the Deposit or the balance thereof after any deductions properly made

6. The Landlord hereby notifies the Tenant under Section 48 of the Landlord & Tenant Act 1987 that any notice (including notices in proceedings) should be served upon the Landlord at the address stated with the name of the Landlord overleaf

7. In the event of damage to or destruction of the Property by any of the risks insured against by the Landlord the Tenant shall be relieved from payment of the Rent to the extent that the Tenant's use and enjoyment of the Property is thereby prevented and from performance of its obligations as to the state and condition of the Property to the extent of and so long as there prevails such damage or destruction (except to the extent that the insurance is prejudiced by any act or default of the Tenant) the amount in case of dispute to be settled by arbitration

8. Where the context so admits:

    8.1 The "Landlord" includes the persons for the time being entitled to the reversion expectant upon this Tenancy

    8.2 The "Tenant" includes any persons deriving title under the Tenant

    8.3 The "Property" includes any part or parts of the Property and all of the Landlord's fixtures and fittings at or upon the Property

    8.4 The "Term" shall mean the period stated in the particulars overleaf or any shorter or longer period in the event of an earlier termination or an extension or holding over respectively

9. All references to the singular shall include the plural and vice versa and any obligations or liabilities of more than one person shall be joint and several and an obligation on the part of a party shall include an obligation not to allow or permit the breach of that obligation

INVENTORY						
Living Room/Lounge	**No.**	**Kitchen/Dining Room**	**No.**	**Bedroom One**	**No.**	**Bedroom Two**
Armchair		Chopping board		Chair		Chair
Chairs		Coffee maker		Chest of drawers		Chest of drawers
Coffee Table		Cups		Curtains		Curtains
Curtains		Dessert spoons		Double bed		Double bed
Framed pictures		Dinner plates		Dressing table		Dressing table
Mirror		Dishwasher		Duvet		Duvet
Net curtains		Draining board		Framed picture		Framed picture
Plant		Egg cups		Lamp		Lamp
Rug		Forks		Mattress cover		Mattress cover
Sofa		Fridge/freezer		Net curtains		Net curtains
Stereo system		Frying pans		Pillow		Pillow
Table		Glasses		Side table		Side table
Table lamp		Kettle		Single bed		Single bed
Telephone		Knives		Table mirror		Table mirror
Television		Microwave		Wallmirror		Wallmirror
		Mugs		Wardrobe		Wardrobe
		Mug tree				
		Oven & hob				
		Pudding /soup dishes				

Bedroom Three	No.	Bathroom/Toilet	No.	Storage Cupboard	No.	
Chair		Basket		Broom		
Chest of drawers		Floor mat		Bucket		
Curtains		Lavatory brush		Clothes horse		
Double bed		Shower curtain		Dustpan & brush		
Dressing table		Soap dish		Iron		
Duvet		Towels		Ironing board		
Framed picture		Wall mirror		Mop		
Lamp		Wooden chair		Vacuum cleaner		
Mattress cover						
Net curtains				**Hall**		
Pillow				Coat stand		
Side table				Framed pictures		
Single bed						
Table mirror						
Vacuum cleaner						
Wallmirror						
Wardrobe						

This Inventory relates to the Property: ……………………………………

If you wish to add any other items to this inventory they should be written on a separate sheet of paper and attached to this Inventory. Both the Landlord and Tenant should sign this Inventory and any additional sheets attached thereto.

Signed.. Signed..

Landlord **Tenant/s**

Dated ....day of...200_.

APPENDIX 3

Notes on completing the form can be found at http://www.wandsworth.gov.uk/planning/plappform1.pdf

---

FORM TP1/94

WANDSWORTH BOROUGH COUNCIL

TOWN & COUNTRY PLANNING ACT 1990
APPLICATION FOR PLANNING PERMISSION

Send the completed form to:-
Borough Planner's Service
The Town Hall
Wandsworth High Street
London
SW18 2PU

For Office Use Only
REF:
FEE PAID:
DATE REC:

(PLEASE READ THE ACCOMPANYING NOTES FOR GUIDANCE AND COMPLETE THE FORM IN BLOCK LETTERS USING BLACK INK)

1 (a) Name and Address of Applicant

1.(b) Name and Address of Agent (if any)

Name for Contact _____

Tel. No _____

Tel. No. _____

Address of Application Site:

2. Description of Proposals:

Have the building works taken place?   YES/NO

4. Type of Application (Please tick box)

A. A full application for new building works (including extensions and other alterations to existing building). ☐

B   A full application for a change of use only. ☐

C. A full application for a change of use <u>and</u> new building works ☐

D   An outline application for new building works (answer question 5) ☐

E   An application for approval of reserved matters of a previous outline permission.
Date of decision and ref. no._____(answer question 6 . ☐

F   An application for removal/variation of condition(s) of a previous planning permission.
Give date of decision and ref. no._____ ☐

G   An application for renewal of a temporary permission. Give date of last decision
and ref. no. _____ ☐

5. Outline Application

If you ticked D in question 4, please tick one or more of these boxes to show which matters <u>are to be considered</u> at this stage.

EXTERNAL APPEARANCE ☐   MEANS OF ACCESS ☐   SITING ☐   LANDSCAPING ☐   DESIGN ☐

6. Reserved Matters

If you ticked F in question 4, please indicate which reserved matters are dealt with in this application.

EXTERNAL APPEARANCE ☐   MEANS OF ACCESS ☐   SITING ☐   LANDSCAPING ☐   DESIGN ☐

7. Drawings

Please list all drawings and any other documents submitted with this application.

8. Site Area and floorspace

(a)   What is the site area in square metres or hectares?   ☐ ha/sq.m

(b)   If the application is for new building works, please give details of:

Existing floorspace.   ☐ sq.m

Proposed floorspace.   ☐ sq.m

(c)   If the proposal is for a change of use, please give details of the amount of floorspace involved.   ☐ sq.m

(d)   Does the proposal involve the removal or demolition of any part of an existing building?   YES/NO

If so, please show on the drawings the extent of the building(s) to be removed.

9. Existing Uses

(a) What is the current use of the site?

(b) If vacant what was it last used for?

(c) If in residential use please state the number of existing:

houses ☐   flats ☐   bedsits ☐

other, please specify

10. If your proposal is for new buildings or extension to an existing building, give details of the make. type and colour of materials to be used on:

(a) Walls

(b) Roof

Details of materials should also be shown on the drawings.

11. Access (Please answer yes / no)

Would the proposal:

(a) involve the provision of a new access for vehicles   _____

(b) the alteration of an existing access for vehicles   _____

(c) the creation or alteration of an access for pedestrians only   _____

12. Trees

Does the proposal involve the felling or pruning of any trees?   _____

If yes, please give details on the submitted plans.

13. Preliminary Discussions: If you have had previous discussions or correspondence with the Council regarding this proposal, please tell us who you spoke to and any reference number quoted by the Council.

TO BE COMPLETED BY ALL APPLICANTS

I apply for planning permission and I enclose (where appropriate) the fee of £ *
by cheque /P.O. No._____ /cash. Cheques and postal orders should be made payable to Wandsworth Borough Council.
If you wish to pay by credit card please ring 020 8871 6636/7

Signed: _____   Date: _____

* *PLEASE SEE GUIDE TO PLANNING FEES*

PLEASE COMPLETE THE APPROPRIATE CERTIFICATE ON THE BACK.

For a freehold property:

SELLER'S PROPERTY INFORMATION FORM

Address of the Property:

....

....

....

IMPORTANT NOTE TO SELLERS

- **Please complete this form carefully. It will be sent to the buyer's solicitor and may be seen by the buyer. If you are unsure how to answer any of the questions, ask your solicitor before doing so.**

- For many of the questions you need only tick the correct answer. Where necessary, please give more detailed answers on a separate sheet of paper. Then send all the replies to your solicitor so that the information can be passed to the buyer's solicitor.

- The answers should be those of the person whose name is on the deeds. If there is more than one of you, you should prepare the answers together.

- It is very important that your answers are correct because the buyer will rely on them in deciding whether to go ahead. Incorrect information given to the buyer through your solicitor, or mentioned to the buyer in conversation between you, may mean that the buyer can claim compensation from you or even refuse to complete the purchase.

- It does not matter if you do not know the answer to any question as long as you say so.

- The buyer will be told by his solicitor that he takes the property as it is. If he wants more information about it, he should get it from his own advisers, not from you.

- If anything changes after you fill in this questionnaire but before the sale is completed, tell your solicitor immediately. This is as important as giving the right answers in the first place.

- Please pass to your solicitor immediately any notices you have received which affect the property. The same goes for notices which arrive at any time before completion.

- If you have a tenant, tell you solicitor immediately there is any change in the arrangements but do nothing without asking your solicitor first.

- You should let your solicitor have any letters, agreements or other documents which help answer the questions. If you know of any which you are not supplying with these answers, please tell your solicitor about them.

- Please complete and return the separate Fixtures, Fittings and Contents Form. It is an important document which will form part of the contract between you and the buyer. Unless you mark clearly on it the items which you wish to remove, they will be included in the sale and you will not be able to take them with you when you move.

Part I – to be completed by the seller

1 Boundaries
"Boundaries" mean any fence, wall, hedge or ditch which marks the edge of your property.

1.1 Looking towards the house from the road, who either owns or accepts responsibility for the boundary:

(a) on the left? WE DO ☐ NEXT DOOR ☐ SHARED ☐ NOT KNOWN ☐

(b) on the right? WE DO ☐ NEXT DOOR ☐ SHARED ☐ NOT KNOWN ☐

(c) at the back? WE DO ☐ NEXT DOOR ☐ SHARED ☐ NOT KNOWN ☐

1.2 If you have answered "not known", which boundaries have you actually repaired or maintained? (Please give details)..
....
....

1.3 Do you know of any boundary being moved in the last 20 years?
(Please give details)..
....
....

2 Disputes
2.1 Do you know of any disputes about this or any neighbouring property?
NO ☐   YES (PLEASE GIVE DETAILS) ☐
....
....

2.2 Have you received any complaints about anything you have, or have not, done as owners?
NO ☐   YES (PLEASE GIVE DETAILS) ☐
....
....

2.3 Have you made any such complaints to any neighbour about what the neighbour has or has not done?

NO ☐   YES (PLEASE GIVE DETAILS) ☐

....

....

3 Notices

3.1 Have you either sent or received any letters or notices which affect your property or the neighbouring property in any way (for example, from or to neighbours, the council or a government department)?

NO ☐   YES ☐   COPIES ENCLOSED ☐   TO FOLLOW ☐   LOST ☐

3.2 Have you had any negotiations or discussions with any neighbour or any local or other authority which affect the property in any way?

NO ☐   YES (PLEASE GIVE DETAILS) ☐

....

....

4 Guarantees

4.1 Are there any guarantees or insurance policies of the following types:

(a) NHBC Foundation 15 or Newbuild?

NO ☐   YES ☐   COPIES ENCLOSED ☐   WITH DEEDS ☐   LOST ☐

(b) Damp course?

NO ☐   YES ☐   COPIES ENCLOSED ☐   WITH DEEDS ☐   LOST ☐

(c) Double glazing?

NO ☐   YES ☐   COPIES ENCLOSED ☐   WITH DEEDS ☐   LOST ☐

(d) Electrical work?

NO ☐   YES ☐   COPIES ENCLOSED ☐   WITH DEEDS ☐   LOST ☐

(e) Roofing?

NO ☐   YES ☐   COPIES ENCLOSED ☐   WITH DEEDS ☐   LOST ☐

(f) Rot or infestation?

NO ☐   YES ☐   COPIES ENCLOSED ☐   WITH DEEDS ☐   LOST ☐

(g) Central heating?

NO ☐   YES ☐   COPIES ENCLOSED ☐   WITH DEEDS ☐   LOST ☐

(h) Anything similar? (e.g. cavity wall insulation)

NO ☐   YES ☐   COPIES ENCLOSED ☐   WITH DEEDS ☐   LOST ☐

(i) Do you have any written details of the work done to obtain any of these guarantees?

NO ☐   YES ☐   COPIES ENCLOSED ☐   WITH DEEDS ☐   LOST ☐

4.2 Have you made or considered making claims under any of these?

NO ☐   YES (PLEASE GIVE DETAILS) ☐

....

....

5 Services

(This section applies to gas, electrical and water supplies, sewerage disposal and telephone cables.)

5.1 Please tick which services are connected to the property.

GAS ☐   ELEC. ☐   WATER ☐   DRAINS ☐   TEL. CABLE ☐   T.V. ☐

5.2 Do any drains, pipes or wires for these cross any neighbour's property?

NOT KNOWN ☐   YES (PLEASE GIVE DETAILS) ☐

....

....

5.3 Do any drains, pipes or wires leading to any neighbour's property cross your property?

NOT KNOWN ☐   YES (PLEASE GIVE DETAILS) ☐

....

....

5.4 Are you aware of any agreement which is not with the deeds about any of these services?

NOT KNOWN ☐   YES (PLEASE GIVE DETAILS) ☐

....

....

6 Sharing with the neighbours

6.1 Are you aware of any responsibility to contribute to the cost of anything used jointly, such as the repair of a shared drive, boundary or drain?

NO ☐   YES (PLEASE GIVE DETAILS) ☐

....

....

6.2 Do you contribute to the cost of repair of anything used by the neighbourhood, such as the maintenance of a private road?

NO ☐   YES ☐

6.3 If so, who is responsible for organising the work and collecting the contributions?

....

....

6.4 Please give details of all such sums paid or owing, and explain if they are paid on a regular basis or only as and when work is required.

....

....

6.5 Do you need to go next door if you have to repair or decorate your building or maintain any of the boundaries?

NO ☐   YES ☐

6.6 If "Yes" have you always been able to do so without objections by the neighbours?

YES ☐   NO (please give details of any objection under the answer to question 2 (disputes))

6.7 Do any of your neighbours need to come onto your land to repair or decorate their building or maintain the boundaries?

NO ☐   YES ☐

6.8 If so, have you ever objected?

NO ☐   YES (please give details of any objection under the answer to question 2)

7 Arrangements and rights

Are there any other formal or informal arrangements which give someone else rights over your property?

NO ☐   YES (PLEASE GIVE DETAILS)

....

....

8 Occupiers

8.1 Does anyone other than you live in the property?

NO ☐   YES ☐

If "No" go to question 9.1
If "Yes" please give their full names and (if under 18) their ages

....

....

8.2 (a)(i) Do any of them have any right to stay on the property with your permission? (These rights may have arisen without you realising, e.g. if they have paid towards the cost of buying the house, paid for improvements or helped you make your mortgage payments.)

NO ☐   YES (PLEASE GIVE DETAILS)

....

....

8.2   (a)(ii) Are any of them tenants or lodgers?

NO ☐   YES (please give details and a copy of any tenancy agreement)

....

....

8.2 (b) Have they all agreed to sign the contract for sale agreeing to leave with you (or earlier)?

NO ☐   YES (PLEASE GIVE DETAILS)

....

....

9 Restrictions

If you have changed the use of the property or carried out any building work on it, please read the note below and answer these questions. If you have not, please go on to Question 10. Note: The title deeds of some properties include clauses which are called "restrictive covenants". For example, these may forbid the owner of the house to carry out any building work or to use it for the purpose of a business – unless someone else (often the builder of the house) gives his consent.

9.1 (a) Do you know of any "restrictive covenant" which applies to your house or land?

NO ☐   YES ☐

(b) If "Yes", did you ask for consent for the work or change of use?

NO ☐   YES (please give details and a copy of a consent)

....

....

9.2 If consent was needed but not obtained, please explain why not

....

....

9.3 If the reply to 9.1(a) is "Yes", please give the name and address of the person from whom consent has to be obtained

....

....

10 Planning

10.1 Is the property used only as a private home?

YES ☐   NO (PLEASE GIVE DETAILS)

....

....

10.2 (a) Is the property a listed building or in a conservation area?

YES ☐   NO ☐   NOT KNOWN ☐

(b) If "Yes" what work has been carried out since it was listed or the area became a conservation area?

....

....

10.3 (a) Has there been any building work on the property in the last four years?

NO ☐   YES (PLEASE GIVE DETAILS)

....

....

(b) If "Yes" was planning permission, building regulation approval or listed building consent obtained?

NO ☐   YES ☐   TO FOLLOW ☐

NOT REQUIRED ☐   COPIES ENCLOSED ☐   LOST ☐

10.4 Have you applied for planning permission, building regulation approval or listed building consent at any time?

NO ☐   YES ☐   COPIES ENCLOSED ☐   TO FOLLOW ☐   LOST ☐

10.5 If "Yes", has any of the work been carried out?

NO ☐   YES (PLEASE GIVE DETAILS)

....

....

10.6 (a) Has there been a change of use of the property in the last 10 years (e.g. dividing into flats, combining flats or using part for business use)?

NO ☐   YES (PLEASE GIVE DETAILS)

....

....

(b) If "Yes", was planning permission obtained?

NO ☐   YES ☐   TO FOLLOW ☐

NOT REQUIRED ☐   COPIES ENCLOSED ☐   LOST ☐

11 Fixtures

11.1 If you have sold through an estate agent, are all items listed in its particulars included in the sale?

NO ☐   YES ☐

If "No" you should contact the estate agent to write to everyone concerned correcting this error.

11.2 Do you own outright everything included in the sale?

YES ☐   NO (PLEASE GIVE DETAILS)

....

....

(You must give details of anything which may not be yours to sell, e.g. anything rented or on H.P.)

12 Expenses

Have you ever had to pay for the use of the property?

YES ☐   NO (PLEASE GIVE DETAILS)

....

....

(Ignore rates, water rates, community charge and gas, electricity and phone bills. Disclose anything else: examples are the clearance of cess pool or septic tank, drainage rate, rent charge.)

13 General

Is there any other information which you think the buyer might have a right to know?

NO ☐   YES (PLEASE GIVE DETAILS)

....

....

Signature(s)

....

....

Date ....

This form is part of The Law Society's TransAction scheme.

For a leasehold property:

SELLER'S LEASEHOLD INFORMATION FORM

Address of the Property:

....
....
....

If you live in leasehold property, please answer the following questions. Some people live in blocks of flats, others in large houses converted into flats and others in single leasehold houses. These questions cover all types of leasehold property, but some of them may not apply to your property. In that case please answer them N/A.

The instructions set out at the front of the Seller's Property Information Form apply to this form as well. Please read them again before giving your answers to these questions.

If you are unsure how to answer any of the questions, ask your solicitor.

PART I – TO BE COMPLETED BY THE SELLER
1 Management Company
    1.1 If there is a management company which is run by the tenants please supply any of the
        following which are in your possession:

    (a) Memorandum and articles of association of the company.
    ENCLOSED ☐   TO FOLLOW ☐   LOST ☐   N/A ☐

    (b) Your share or membership certificate.
    ENCLOSED ☐   TO FOLLOW ☐   LOST ☐   N/A ☐

    c) The management accounts for the last 3 years.
    ENCLOSED ☐   TO FOLLOW ☐   LOST ☐   N/A ☐

    (d) Copy of any regulations made by either the landlord or the company additional to the rules
        contained in the lease.
    ENCLOSED ☐   TO FOLLOW ☐   LOST ☐   N/A ☐

    (e) The names and addresses of the secretary and treasurer of the company.
    ....
    ....

This form is part of The Law Society's TransAction scheme.

Resources

Building material and information

THE BUILDING CENTRE
26 Store Street
London WC1E 7BT
Tel: 0906 5 16 11 36
www.buildingcentre.co.uk
Information on everything to do with building and building materials. Offers advice to members of the public about general building enquiries.

COUNCIL FOR REGISTERED GAS INSTALLERS (CORGI)
4 Elmwood
Chineham Business Park
Crockford Lane
Basingstoke
Hants RG24 8WG
Tel: 01256 372 200
www.corgi-gas.com
(All gas installers must be CORGI-registered.)

CRAFTS COUNCIL INFORMATION UNIT
44a Pentonville Road
London N1 9BY
Tel: 020 7278 7700
www.craftscouncil.org.uk
National organisation for promoting contemporary crafts. Apply for the Index of Selected Makers, which lists craftsmen and women with experience and a good reputation.

DESIGN COUNCIL
28 Haymarket
London W1Y 4SU
Tel: 020 7420 5200
www.design-council.org.uk/design
Houses a permanent display of well-designed British products, and an index of modern consumer products.

DYNO-LOCKS AND DYNO-ROD
Zockoll House
143 Maple Road
Surbiton
Surrey KT6 4BJ
Tel: 020 8481 2200
www.dyno-rod.com
Nationwide emergency lock and drain service.

ELECTRICAL CONTRACTORS ASSOCIATION LTD
Esca House
34 Palace Court
London W2 4JG
Tel: 020 7313 4800
www.eca.co.uk
Publishes a list of members.

FEDERATION OF MASTER BUILDERS
Gordon Fisher House
14–15 Great James Street
London WC1N 3DP
Tel: 020 7242 7583
www.fmb.org.uk
Contact regional offices for lists of members; admits only experienced builders.

GAS CONSUMER'S COUNCIL
Abford House
15 Wilton Road
London SW1V 1LT
Tel: 020 7931 0977
Offers independent advice and help to British Gas customers as well as third-party suppliers.

THE HEATING VENTILATION CONTRACTORS' ASSOCIATION
Esca House
34 Palace Court
London W2 4JG
Tel: 020 7313 4900
www.hvca.org.uk

INSTITUTE OF PLUMBING
64 Station Lane
Hornchurch
Essex RM12 6NB
Tel: 01708 472791
www.plumbers.org.uk
Publishes a list of members.

NATIONAL ASSOCIATION OF PLUMBING HEATING AND MECHANICAL SERVICES
Ensign House, Ensign Business Centre
Westwood Way
Coventry CV4 8JA
Tel: 0800 5426060
www.aphc.co.uk
Publishes a list of members.

NATIONAL TILE ASSOCIATION
39 Upper Elmers End Road
Beckenham
Kent BR3 3QY
Tel: 020 8663 0946
Freephone (for UK users only): 0800 783 8886
www.nta.org.uk
Publishes a list of members.

PAINTING AND DECORATING FEDERATION
Construction House
56–64 Leonard House
London EC2A 4JX
Tel: 020 7608 5093
www.painting-decorating-federation.org.uk
Publishes a list of members.

NATIONAL FEDERATION OF
ROOFING CONTRACTORS
24 Weymouth Street
London W1N 3FA
Tel: 020 7435 0387
www.nfrc.co.uk
Publishes a list of members.

NATIONAL HOUSE BUILDING COUNCIL
Registered Office
Buildmark House
Chiltern Avenue
Amersham
Bucks HP6 5AP
Tel: 01494 735363
www.nhbc.co.uk
*Publishes a list of members and registers newly
built houses.*

RENTOKIL INITIAL PLC
Felcourt
East Grinstead
Sussex RH19 2JY
Tel: 01342 833022
www.rentokil-initial.com
*Operates guaranteed service for the eradication of
dry rot and woodworm. Pest Control Division will also
get rid of pests.*

Paint

AMERON INTERNATIONAL
Bankside
Hull HU5 1SQ
Tel: 01482 341441
www.ameroninternational.co.uk

COURTAULDS COATINGS
50 George Street
London W1A 2BB
Tel: 020 7474 1939

DULUX
ICI Paints plc
Wexham Road
Slough
Berks SL2 5DS
Tel: 01753 550555
www.dulux.co.uk

HARLEQUIN FABRICS AND
WALLCOVERINGS
Ladybird House
Beeches Road
Loughborough
Leics LE11 2HA
Tel: 01509 225000
www.harlequin.uk.com

FARROW & BALL
Uddens Estate
Wimborne
Dorset BH21 7NL
Tel: 01202 876141

PAPERS AND PAINTS LTD
4 Park Walk
London SW10 0AD
Tel: 020 7352 8626
www.colourman.com
*Specialises in 18th- and 19th-century paint colour,
plus full range of modern paints.*

Tile and stone

AL-MURAD
Barclay Square
Scotter Road
Scunthorpe DN16 7EJ
Tel: 01724 875000

BRITISH CERAMIC TILE COUNCIL
Federation House, Station Road
Stoke-on-Trent
Staffs ST4 2RT
Tel: 01782 747147

CAESAR'S CERAMICS
358 Edgware Road
London W2 1EB
Tel: 020 72249671

CORRES MEXICAN TILES
15 Ewer Street
London SE1 0NR
Tel: 020 7261 0941

DOMUS TILES
33 Parkgate Road
London SW11 4NP
Tel: 0845 062 5555
www.domustiles.co.uk

FIRED EARTH TILES PLC
Twyford Mill
Oxford Road
Adderbury
Oxon OX17 3HP
Tel: 01295 814315
www.firedearth.co.uk

FOCUS CERAMICS LTD
Unit 4, Hamm Moor Lane
Weybridge Trading Estate
Weybridge
Surrey KT15 2SF
Tel: 01932 854881
www.focusceramics.com

LANGLEY LONDON LTD
161–167 Borough High Street
London SE1 1HU
Tel: 020 7407 4444
Tiles and glass blocks.

THE LIFE-ENHANCING TILE COMPANY
Unit 3B, Central Trading Estate
Bath Road
Bristol BS4 3EH
Tel: 0117 977 4600
www.letco.demon.co.uk

PILKINGTON'S TILES LTD
Rake Lane
PO Box 4
Clifton Junction
Manchester M27 2LP
Tel: 0161 727 1000
www.pilkingtons.com
*Glazed and unglazed ceramic floor and wall tiles;
bathroom accessories.*

PORCELANOSA
The Carr Carriage Drive
Doncaster DN4 5NT
Tel: 01302 341029

RYE TILES
The Old Brewery
Wish Ward
Rye
Kent TN31 7DH
Tel: 01797 233038

TERRA FIRMA TILES
70 Chalk Farm Road
London NW1 8AN
Tel: 020 7485 7227
www.terrafirmatiles.co.uk

TILESTYLE LTD
89–90 North Wall Quay
Dublin
Tel: 03531 855 5200
www.tilestyle.ie

WORLD'S END TILES
Silverthorne Road
London SW8 3HE
Tel: 020 7819 2110
www.worldsendtiles.co.uk

 Carpets and flooring

ALTRO FLOORS
Works Road
Letchworth
Herts SG6 1NW
Tel: 01462 480480
www.altro.co.uk
Rubber flooring.

THE AMTICO COMPANY
Solar Park, Southside
Solihull
West Midlands B90 4NZ
Tel: 0121 745 0800
www.amtico.com

CARPETRIGHT
Amberley House
New Road
Rainham
Essex RM13 8QN
www.carpetright.co.uk

CARPET TILE CENTRES
227 Woodhouse Road
London N12 9BD
Tel: 020 8361 1261

ENGLISH WOODLANDS TIMBER
Cocking Sawmills
Cocking
Midhurst
West Sussex GU29 0HS
Tel: 01730 816941

THE HARDWOOD FLOORING COMPANY
146/152 West End Lane
London NW6 1SD
Tel: 020 7328 8481
www.hardwoodflooringcompany.com
New and reclaimed hardwood floors and worktops.

HERITAGE WOODCRAFT
Heritage House
Wheatfield Way
Hinckley Fields Industrial Estate
Leics LE10 1YG
Tel: 01455 890800
www.woodfloor.co.uk

INTERFACE FLOORING SYSTEMS LTD
Shelf Mills
Halifax
West Yorkshire HX3 7PA
Tel: 01274 690690
Tiles: tufted, fusion bonded, fibre bonded.

KAHRS UK
Unit 2 West
68 Bognor Road
Chichester
West Sussex P019 2NS
Tel: 01243 778747
www.kahrs.com
Specialists in pre-finished laminated flooring.

SINCLAIR TILL
793 Wandsworth Road
London SW8 3JQ
Tel: 020 7720 0031
Linoleum.

STONELL
Forstal House
Beltring
Paddock Wood
Kent TN12 6PY
Tel: 01892 833500
www.stonell.com
Natural slate flooring.

THE WEST SUSSEX ANTIQUE
TIMBER COMPANY
Reliance Works
Newpound
Wisborough Green
West Sussex RH14 0AZ
Tel: 01403 700139
www.wsatimber.co.uk
Salvage specialists also offering new floors with an 'antique' finish.

WEAVER FLOORING
7 Bargate
Newark
Notts NG24 1ES
Tel: 01636 701193

 Windows

ANGLIAN WINDOWS
(Commercial Division)
114–118 Oak Street
Norwich NR3 3BP
Tel: 0800 500 600
www.anglianhome.co.uk

EVEREST LTD
Everest House
Sopers Road
Cuffley
Potters Bar
Herts EN6 4SG
Tel: 01707 875700
www.everest.co.uk

HOMESEAL
15 Homes Drive
Eastern Green
Coventry CV5 7DH
Contact: Paul Redmond
Tel: 02476 466260/ 07976 710463

THE ORIGINAL BOX SASH WINDOW CO.
29–30 The Arches
Alma Road
Windsor
Berks SL4 1QZ
Tel: Freephone 0800 783 4053
www.boxsash.com

Finding your property online

www.assertahome.com
www.fish4homes.co.uk
www.homehunter.co.uk
www.home-to-home.co.uk
www.numberone4property.co.uk
www.primelocation.com
www.propertyfinder.co.uk
www.propertylocator.co.uk
www.reallymoving.com
www.themovechannel.com
www.thisislondon.co.uk
www.ukhomesguide.co.uk

Finding your mortgage online

www.e-mortgages-uk.com
www.firstmortgage.co.uk
www.loanspage.co.uk
www.non-status-mortgage.co.uk
www.yourmortgage.co.uk

Kitchen suppliers

MAIN NATIONAL SUPPLIERS

All sites have building advice, online product search and store locator.

B&Q
www.diy.com

HOMEBASE
www.homebase.co.uk

MFI
www.mfi.co.uk

MOBEN
www.moben.co.uk

POGGENPOHL
www.poggenpohl.co.uk

WELLMAN
www.wellman.co.uk

WICKES
www.wickes.co.uk

OTHER KITCHEN SUPPLIERS

ARLINGTON KITCHENS
Arlington Works, Arlington Road
East Twickenham
Middlesex TW1 2BB
Tel: 020 8892 9803
www.arlingtonkitchens.co.uk
Specialists in designing, manufacturing and installing traditional and contemporary kitchens.

BA KITCHEN COMPONENTS
DERRYLORAN INDUSTRIAL ESTATE
Cookstown
Co. Tyrone
Northern Ireland BT80 9LU
www.bakitchencomponent.com
Range of accessories and doors for kitchen and bedroom units to trade customers in UK and Ireland.

CHANTRY KITCHENS
Unit 7, Centre Park
Marston Business Park, Rudgate
Tockwith, Nr. York YO26 7QF
Tel: 01423 358882
www.chantrykitchens.co.uk
Suppliers and manufacturers of bespoke kitchens.

CHARISMA KITCHENS
11 High Street
Tunbridge Wells
Tel: 01892 532228
www.charismakitchens.co.uk
Offers a professional, personal kitchen fitting service.

CHRISTOPHER HOWARD CABINET MAKERS
The Old Dairy
6 Hall Crescent
Gullane
East Lothian
Scotland EH31 2HA
Tel: 01620 842741
www.christopherhoward.com
Exclusive bespoke kitchens hand built in Scotland with innovative design.

CONTROLLED INTERIORS
Unit 2, Albany Business Centre
Wickham Road
Fareham, Hants PO17 5BD
Tel: 01329 825932
www.controlled-interiors.co.uk
Specialists in the design, manufacture and installation of hand-made kitchens, bedrooms and home-office furniture.

CUSTOM INTERIORS
5–7 Lawrence Lane
Eccleston, Chorley
Lancs PR7 5SJ
Tel: 01257 450413
www.custominteriors.co.uk
Offer a range of kitchens, home furnishings, fitted bedrooms, bathrooms and office studies.

ELITE TRADE KITCHENS LTD
90–92 Willesden Lane
London NW6 7TA
Tel: 020 7328 1234
www.elitekitchens.co.uk
English kitchens, including base and wall units, worktops and kitchen appliances. Supplied for a single dwelling or complete housing estate.

EXPRESS KITCHEN DISTRIBUTION
Unit 2, Camp Street
Bornmore Industrial Estate
Bury, Lancs BL8 1NR
Tel: 0161 797 6665
www.expresskitchens.co.uk
Supplies kitchens and appliances to the trade, either on supply-only basis or including a professional fitting service.

GREENWICH WOOD WORKS
Friendly Place
Lewisham Road
London SE13 7QS
Tel: 020 8694 8449
www.greenwichwoodworks.co.uk
Hand-built kitchens and furniture from London-based workshop.

HABITAT
196 Tottenham Court Road
London W1T
Tel: 020 76313880
Offers kitchen appliances as well as a range of other home furnishings.

HOMESTYLE LUXURY FITTED KITCHENS
8 Victoria Mill
Leeds Street
Wigan WN3 4BW
Tel: 0845 642 4295
www.homestylekitchens.co.uk
Offers kitchens, doors and accessories to the trade and general public.

IN-TOTO
Shaw Cross Court
Shaw Cross Business Park
Dewsbury
West Yorks WF12 7RF
Tel: 01924 487900
www.intoto.co.uk
Range of contemporary and traditional fitted kitchens. Product and showroom details.

MARTIN INTERIORS
The Clocktower
Bargate
Newark
Notts NG24 1ES
Tel: 01636 605118
www.martininteriors.co.uk
Suppliers of fitted kitchens and kitchen appliances.

MERCHANT CITY DISTRIBUTORS
21 St Bryde Street
The Village
East Kilbride G74 4HQ
Tel: 01355 266683
www.merchantcitydistributors.co.uk
Trade suppliers of kitchens, domestic appliances, sinks and lighting.

PAULA ROSA
Water Lane
Storrington
West Sussex RH20 3DS
Tel: 01903 746666
www.paularosa.co.uk
Design, manufacture and installation of kitchens. Showrooms throughout the UK.

PLAIN AND SIMPLE KITCHENS
332 Deansgate
Manchester M3 4LY
Tel: 0161 839 8983
www.ps4kitchens.co.uk
Supplier and installer of kitchens with a nationwide service.

RE-NU KITCHENS
60 Nuffield Road
Nuffield Industrial Estate
Poole, Dorset BH17 0RT
Tel: 01202 687642
www.re-nukitchens.co.uk
Supplier and installer of replacement cabinet doors.

ROBERT WOODS DESIGN
The Old Station, Station Yard
Harmby Road
Leyburn
North Yorks DL8 5ET
Tel: 01969 622131
www.mywebpage.net/robertwoods
Portfolio site from makers of bespoke fitted kitchens and cabinets.

ROBINSON INTERIORS
10 Boucher Way
Belfast BT12 6RE
Tel: 028 906 83838
www.robinsoninteriors.com
UK and Ireland kitchen and bedroom design, bespoke and contemporary interiors and appliances.

SPACE SAVERS
222 Kentish Town Road
London NW5 2AD
www.spacesaver.co.uk
Unique kitchens. Small spaces a speciality.

STRICKLAND INTERIOR DESIGN
Tel: 07799 417803
www.strickland–interior–design.com
Specialists in contemporary interior design.

STEVIAN KITCHENS AND BEDROOMS
Unit 8, West Chirton Industrial Estate (South)
Norham Road
North Shields
Tyne & Wear NE29 7EY
Tel: 0191 296 1130
www.steviankitchens.co.uk
Manufacturers of fitted unit carcasses for custom-made kitchens and bedrooms.

WE PLAN KITCHENS
www.weplankitchens.com
Professional kitchen design and remodelling service. Features ful CAD and online design service.

WOODSTOCK
4 William Street
London SW1X 9HL
Tel: 020 7245 9989
www.woodstockfurniture.co.uk
Bespoke furniture for kitchens and other rooms.

 Information on converting old and listed buildings into residential properties

ASBESTOS REMOVAL
Davis Environmental Ltd
Head Office
Church farm
Hospital Lane
Warwickshire CV12 0J2
Tel: 07976 684717

THE DEPARTMENT OF CULTURE, MEDIA AND SPORT (LISTED BUILDINGS)
Tel: 020 7211 6200
www.culture.gov.uk/heritage/index.html

ENGLISH HERITAGE
Customer Services Department
PO Box 569
Swindon
SN2 2YP
Tel: 0870 333 1181
www.english-heritage.org.uk

THE GEORGIAN GROUP
6 Fitzroy Square
London W1P 6DX
Tel: 020 7387 1720
www.heritage.co.uk/georgian

THE RAVEN GROUP
21 Knightsbridge
London SW1X 7LY
Tel: 020 7235 0422

SAVE BRITAIN'S HERITAGE
70 Cowcross Street
London EC1M 6EJ
Tel: 020 7253 3500
www.savebritainsheritage.org/main.htm

THE SOCIETY FOR THE PROTECTION OF ANCIENT BUILDINGS
37 Spital Square
London E1 6DY
Tel: 020 7377 1644
www.spab.org.uk

THE VICTORIAN SOCIETY
1 Priory Gardens
Bedford Park
London W4 1TT
Tel: 020 8994 1019
www.victorian-society.org.uk

Index

Author's acknowledgments

With special thanks to:
Sarah Walmsley, Matt Baker, Johanna Fry, Katie D'Souza, Elizabeth Assaf, Charlotte Bennett, Caroline Beeny, Richard and Tricia Beeny, Phillips Solicitors, Bell Associates, Copplestones Unsworth and Co., Linda Marsh, MFI, Letonthenet.co.uk, www.sliceinteractive.co.uk (website design), strickland_interior_design.com, Liberty Godwin at Plain English (bespoke kitchens and furniture), Geoffrey Pidgeon, chairman of Original Bathrooms, Cavendish Mortgage Brokers, Laura Hill, Fiona Screen, Mal Peachey, Katie Cowan, Barbara Saulini and Cat Ledger.

And to all those who created the series *Property Ladder*:
Philippa Ransford, John Silver, Ben Frow, Daisy Goodwin, Caroline McCool, Ita Fitzgerald, Ian Barnes, Victoria Watson, Alexandra Cox, Dan Dimbleby, Melany Hunt, Sarah Delafield-Cook, Craig Pickles, Charlotte Bennett, Steve Rees, Karen Shipway, Graeme Strong, Eskimo, Kyriacos Santorini, Skaramoosh, Evolutions, Jonnie Case, Tristram Harris, Jo Abercrombie, Polly Rose, David Langan, Robin Cox, Paul Kerrigan, Laurie Rose, Lucy Shanahan, Gemma Shanley, Zoe Goodchild, Perry Harrison, Ian Liddington, Nina Somers, Sarah Walmsley, Michael Douglas, Jenny Freilich, Nat Sharman, Ceri Rowlands, Donna McLaughlin, Matt Baker, Johanna Fry, Katie D'Souza, Elizabeth Assaf, Charlotte Bennett, Oscar Challis, Michael Wood, James Worby, Lindsey Crisp, Magpie Films, Chris Evans, Stephen Hart, Raysan Al Kubaisi, Paul Steiner, Tony Pound, Lorraine Want, James Cooper, Graeme Dawson and Leila Farag.

Photos of Sarah: Laurence Cendrowicz

Lincoln photos pages 66 to 71: Roger Mockford @ Roger Mockford Photography Ltd, Lincoln, Tel: 01522 693 333

Garden design page 117: Linda Marsh Landscape Design

Illustrations pages 77 and 80: Dave Chipping at Floorplanners

Illustration page 99: Barbara Saulini

Forms on pages 148 to 154 reproduced by kind permission of Letonthenet; pages 158 to 165 by the Law Society.